The Animal Things
We Say

THE
ANIMAL THINGS
WE SAY

by
Darryl Lyman

Foreword by
Richard A. Spears

Associate Professor of Linguistics,
Northwestern University

J**D** JONATHAN DAVID PUBLISHERS, INC.
MIDDLE VILLAGE, NEW YORK 11379

Jonathan David Publishers, Inc.
68-22 Eliot Avenue
Middle Village, New York 11379

10 9 8 7 6 5 4 3 2 1

Library of Congress Cataloging in Publication Data

Lyman, Darryl, 1944-
    The animal things we say.

    Bibliography: p.
    Includes index.
    1. English language—Etymology—Glossaries,
vocabularies, etc. 2. English language—Terms and
phrases. 3. Animals—Miscellanea. 4. Zoology—
Nomenclature (Popular) I. Title.
PE1583.L9   1982   422   82-10026
ISBN 0-8246-0291-9   AACR2

Printed in the United States of America

To my niece
LISA

Contents

PART TWO

Foreword

I suggest that you take a reading trip through Darryl Lyman's fascinating menagerie of "animalisms." You will learn as much about humans as about animals. You will see evidence of the human intellect at work drawing upon the animal world for imagery. You will also see the human intellect at work dreaming up logical rationalizations for fanciful figures of speech. If you like words and their histories, and if you are interested in animals, especially human ones, you will surely enjoy your trip through this linguistic zoo.

Readers interested in the history of the English language will be delighted that Mr. Lyman has included thorough word histories of each animal word discussed. These etymologies show the origin of the animal name and its Latin, Scandinavian, Greek, Modern German, French, and Modern English forms. In some instances, it is clear that the English-speaking peoples have borrowed animal words and expressions ready-made from foreign languages.

Language and folklore buffs will also be rewarded by the fascinating origins proposed by Mr. Lyman for the expressions in this collection. Many of the origins are based in folklore of a very special kind. That is the human need to explain the origins of words. There is a need to dignify words, even homemade words, with a pedigree or at least a plausible explanation or origin. Many of these explanations are just as creative and as much a part of fantasy as the animalisms themselves.

In *The Animal Things We Say*, Darryl Lyman presents hundreds of expressions that recall for us our traditional connection with nature, especially our relationship with other forms of animal life.

Richard A. Spears

Associate Professor
of Linguistics,
Northwestern University

Introductory Note

Animals have helped humans in many ways. One service, however, is seldom mentioned—the way animals have enriched human language. From ancient times to the present, people have drawn upon the animal world for imagery to express all sorts of emotions and ideas. However, until now these rich language resources have not been examined as a body.

The purpose of this book is to explore many of the animal things we say. The material selected for inclusion consists of a broad range of words and phrases that are animal-related in origin but that are often used in transferred or figurative senses. Words commonly listed as vulgar or slang are (with a few exceptions) not included, because such words are voluminous and are adequately covered in slang dictionaries. The emphasis here is on standard and colloquial expressions.

Some expressions are based on an animal's appearance; others, on an animal's habits. Some are based on a positive feeling about an animal; others, on a negative feeling. Some are based on true characteristics of an animal; others, on false beliefs. Some expressions have a clear, definite origin; others, an uncertain origin buried in the dim past.

Part One covers expressions that are based on the names of animals (*ant, hare, toad*), the names of animal body parts *(beak, paw, rumen)*, and the names of things that animals produce with their bodies *(cobweb, honey, wax)*.

Part Two covers expressions that are based on other types of animal-related words and phrases, such as the names of animal groups *(brood, flock, herd)*, the names of animal homes *(burrow, den, nest)*, and expressions in which no actual animal words are used *(beat about the bush, constable, one fell swoop)*.

Part One

Albatross

The English word *albatross* for a type of seabird has evolved from a strange mixture of several languages. Its immediate source is the earlier English word *alcatras*. *Alcatras*, however, was originally applied to a different type of seabird, the black frigate bird. When seamen began inaccurately to apply the name *alcatras*, or sometimes *algatross*, to a larger, usually white bird, the word gradually changed to *albatross* under the influence of the Latin word *albus* ("white").

The earlier English form of *alcatras* itself is an alteration of Spanish and Portuguese *alcatraz* ("pelican"), a variant of Portuguese *alcatruz* ("bucket of a waterwheel"), which comes from Arabic *al-qadus* ("the water jar"), which in turn goes back to Hebrew *kad* ("water jar, bucket"). The albatross, then, is "the white water-carrier." Note, however, that the "water-carrier" part is really not accurate, because that idea was originally applied to the huge bill of the pelican and was transferred to the albatross by mistake.

albatross around one's neck

The albatross is any one of various web-footed birds, including the largest of seabirds. Albatross feathers may be brown, black and white, or almost all white. A master at gliding, the albatross can stay aloft on virtually motionless wings for many hours at a time. For that reason, seamen used to believe that the albatross has magical powers and that disaster or death would haunt anyone who kills the bird.

In 1798 the great English poet Samuel Taylor Coleridge made that belief the basis for his famous poem "The Rime of the Ancient Mariner." The Ancient Mariner (that is, the "old seaman") tells the story of how he, while on a ship at sea, killed an albatross for no apparent reason. Later the breeze stopped blowing, and the ship could not reach port to get fresh water. The crew assumed that the bad luck came because of the death of the albatross. Angry at the Ancient Mariner, the crew picked up the dead bird and hung it around the man's neck as a symbol of guilt and punishment.

Today anything that causes worry or trouble is often called an *albatross*. And because of Coleridge's poem, a common way of saying that one has a serious problem is to say that there is an *albatross around one's neck.*

Alligator

When early Spanish explorers landed in the New World, they found a reptile so huge that they called it simply *el lagarto* ("the lizard"). In English, *el lagarto* was soon modified to *allagarto* and various other forms before finally settling on *alligator*. Spanish *el lagarto* itself goes back to Latin *lacertus* ("lizard"), which is related to *lacertus* ("muscle," originally the muscular part of the upper arm), which is based on an Indo-European root meaning "limb." The lizard, hence the alligator, is named for its muscular appearance.

alligator

Sometimes paint or varnish will crack, as from having applied it incorrectly or from ordinary weathering. The cracked appearance reminds many people of the rough hide of an alligator. When such cracking happens, the paint or varnish is said *to alligator.*

In American slang, a tough man, being compared to the fearsome reptile, used to be called an *alligator.* Later the term referred simply to a hep, swaggering male, specifically an enthusiastic fan of swing music. From the swing use of *alligator* comes the familiar expression *see you later, alligator* (meaning goodbye), to which another person usually responds with *after while, crocodile* (also meaning goodbye). Each expression is based on a simple rhyming pattern. The second one uses *crocodile* simply because the first one uses *alligator*, the two animals being closely related.

alligator clip

Temporary electrical connections can be made with a clip that has jagged teeth and long, narrow jaws. The device, because of its appearance, is called an *alligator clip*.

alligator pear

The avocado is a well-known pear-shaped fruit. The edible part inside the skin is usually soft and light green, but the dark skin itself is, in some varieties, coarse and bumpy. Partly from the appearance of the skin and partly because of mispronunciation of the earlier forms of the word (such as *avigato*), the avocado is sometimes called the *alligator pear*.

see you later, alligator

(See *alligator* above.)

Ant

The Modern English word *ant* for a type of insect comes from Middle English *ante* ("ant"), which goes back through the forms *amte* and *amete* to Old English *aemete* ("ant"). *Aemete* is composed of two parts: *ae-* (an Old English prefix meaning "off") and *-mete* (derived from an unrecorded Old English verb, of Indo-European origin, meaning "to cut"). The ant, then, is "the cutter-off" or "the biter-off."

have ants in one's pants

If ants, as "cutters-off" or "biters-off," got inside someone's clothing, they would probably cause the person to become suddenly active. From that idea has developed a common expression: to be impatient or eager to act or speak is *to have ants in one's pants*.

Ape

Ape refers to any member of a family of large, tailless Old World primates, such as the gorilla or the chimpanzee. Loosely, *ape* is used to mean any monkey. The Modern English word *ape* goes back to Old English *apa* ("ape"). The ultimate origin of *ape* is uncertain. Some authorities take the word back to Common Germanic, others to Old Slavic *apica* ("ape"). But the true origin might be hinted at in Egyptian *aafi* ("a hideous man") and *gafi, gef* ("ape"). If, however, *ape* is, as conjectured by some, "the imitator," then a Celtic origin is possible; compare Gaelic *atharrais* ("a mimic") and Manx *arrish* ("mimicry, a mimic").

ape

It was long ago noticed that apes have a tendency to imitate human actions. Therefore, among humans, to imitate or mimic is *to ape* or *to play the ape.*

A large, uncouth person is sometimes called an *ape.*

go ape over

Apes are also known for their uninhibited displays of emotion. Thus, to be extremely enthusiastic about something is *to go ape over* it.

Ass

The English word *ass* for the donkey goes back to Latin *asinus* ("ass").

asinine

(See *ass* below.)

ass

The ass is a long-eared patient animal, similar to the horse but smaller. The ass has long been used as a beast of burden, that is, an animal that carries heavy objects. Since the days of the ancient Greeks, the ass has been generally called clumsy and stupid. It is common, then, to refer to a clumsy, foolish person as an *ass.*

English *asinine,* meaning foolish, comes from the same source, Latin *asinus* ("ass").

make an ass of oneself

To do something foolish is *to make an ass of oneself.*

Baboon

The English word *baboon* for a type of primate goes back to Old French *babuin* ("baboon"), which is a blend of *baboue* ("grimace, ugly face") and *babine* ("the lip of certain animals, especially monkeys"—because the baboon has prominent lips). *Baboue* and *babine,* both of which are associated with the notion of making incoherent speech sounds, are based on an Indo-European root imitative of unarticulated or indistinct speech. The baboon is literally "the ugly animal with big lips."

baboon

A coarse person, especially one of low intelligence, is sometimes called a *baboon,* commonly a "big *baboon.*"

Badger

The word *badger* for a type of burrowing mammal probably refers to the white mark, or badge, on the animal's forehead. *Bauson,* an earlier (French-derived) word for the animal, is based on the same reference.

badger

In England, there used to be a cruel sport called badgerbaiting (see *bait* under "Animal-related Expressions" in Part Two), which involved the use of dogs to bait, or torment, the animal. Hence, among humans, to tease, annoy, harass, or torment is *to badger.*

badger game

There is a human version of badgerbaiting. In this case,

the victim is a man, and the dogs are a couple of black-mailers. The "game" is a criminal scheme in which a woman invites a man to make amorous advances toward her and then forces him to pay money when her male accomplice, posing as her husband, enters and threatens violence or scandal. This scheme is called the *badger game*. Now any form of blackmail, extortion, intimidation, or deception for personal gain can be called a *badger game*.

Bantam

The word *bantam* for a type of small fowl is derived from the name of the little village of Bantam, in Java, where the animal was believed to have originated.

bantam

The male bantam is a fierce fighter. In cockfights, it has been known to defeat much larger gamecocks. A person who is small but courageous or quarrelsome is often called a *bantam* or a *bantam rooster*.

bantamweight

In professional boxing, a fighter weighing from 113 to 118 pounds is called a *bantamweight*.

Bat

The word *bat* for a mouselike nocturnal flying mammal is not the original English name for the animal. The Old English word for the bat is *hreremus* ("shaking mouse"), obviously because of the "shaking" movement of the bat's wings. Modern German still uses a similar word, *Fledermaus* ("bat," literally "flutter mouse"). But the Modern English word *bat* comes from Middle English *bakke* ("bat"), which is probably adapted from a Scandinavian language. Old Danish, for example, has *nathbakkae* ("night bat"), which goes back to Old Norse *ledhrblaka* ("bat," literally "leather-flutterer" or "leather-flapper"); Old Norse *blaka* ("to flutter, flap") is based on an Indo-European root meaning "to strike." The bat, then, is originally "the flutterer" or "the flapper."

bat

A prostitute, like a bat, usually has nocturnal habits. Therefore, one of the slang terms for a prostitute is *bat*. *Bat* also stands for an unpleasant woman or is simply used as a general term of abuse toward another person.

bat house

An insane asylum is called a *bat house*. *Bat* is here derived from *bats* and *batty* (see *bats, batty* below).

bats, batty

Bats and *batty* are shortened versions of *have bats in the belfry* (see *have bats in the belfry* below).

blind as a bat

Contrary to popular belief, all species of bats can see. It is true, however, that many bats can see only poorly and that sonar is their main method of avoiding dashing their brains out against walls. Therefore, there is some justification for saying that a person who can see little or nothing is *(as) blind as a bat*.

have bats in the belfry

The belfry is that part of a church tower where the bells are hung. Bats have been known to go into the belfry and fly about crazily. Since the belfry, as the upper part of a church, suggests a person's head, it is said that to be crazy or foolish (in the head, of course) is *to have bats in the* (or *one's*) *belfry*.

like a bat out of hell

The bat, being a nocturnal animal, is associated with darkness. Therefore, in the folklore of many parts of the world, it is said that the devil, the Prince of Darkness, often takes the form of a bat. In fact, the devil is often depicted with bat's wings. Bats are also generally associated with caves, which look like routes to hell, the devil's habitat. Bats are also noted for their quick, darting flight. All of these associations have come together in a twentieth-century expression: to go very quickly is to go *like a bat out of hell*.

Beak

The Modern English word *beak* for the bill of a bird comes from Middle English *bek, bec* ("beak"), which derive from Old French *bec* ("beak"), which comes from Late Latin *beccus* ("beak"), itself of Gaulish origin and probably related to a Celtic word meaning "a point" or "a hook." The animal beak, then, is probably named for its typically pointed appearance.

beak

A person's nose is sometimes humorously referred to as a *beak*. In fact, anything that looks like a bird's bill, such as the spout of a water pitcher, can be called a *beak*.

Bear

The Modern English word *bear* for a type of large mammal goes back to Old English *bera* ("bear"), which is based on an Indo-European root meaning "brown." The bear, then, is originally "the brown animal."

angry as a bear

To be extremely angry is to be *(as) angry* (or *cross*) *as a bear*.

be a bear for (punishment)

Because of the bear's strength and endurance, a person who is capable of, and eager for, any kind of effort is said *to be a bear for* it. To be rugged, determined, and able to withstand rough treatment is *to be a bear for punishment* (or *hard work*).

bear

Because of the bear's occasional fierceness, a rough, rude, or clumsy person is sometimes called a *bear*.

A person having special ability, enthusiasm, or ruggedness is also a *bear* (as in *be a bear for* above). Related to the latter is *bear* meaning a difficult task.

bear and bull

In business, a person who sells stock before he himself

actually owns it is called a *bear*. It is believed that this term comes from the old expression *to sell the bearskin before the bear is caught.*

A *bear* is also someone who, expecting the price to fall, sells his stock in order to buy it back later at a lower price. This sense of the word may come from the idea that a bear attacks by sweeping its paws downward (suggesting the downward move in the price).

A *bull*, on the other hand, buys stock in the belief that the price will rise and that the value of his stock will increase. This expression may come from the bull's method of attacking by tossing its head and horns upward (suggesting the upward move in the price).

bear hug

The bear is known for its fighting tactic of wrapping its arms around a victim and squeezing. Among humans, then, a tight, though usually affectionate, embrace is called a *bear hug*. In wrestling, a *bear hug* is a similar move but without the affection—the aim is to throw the opponent on his back.

loaded for bear

Beginning in the late 1800s, to be drunk was to be "loaded" (with liquor). Punning this *loaded* with the *loaded* that describes a weapon having an explosive charge, the expression expanded to *loaded for bear*, still meaning drunk. That sense has faded, but the colorful expression itself has survived with new meanings based on further extensions of the loaded-weapon image. Today, then, to be well prepared or very angry (that is, prepared for a fight) is to be *loaded for bear.*

Beast

The English word *beast* for an animal goes back to Latin *bestia* ("beast").

beast

A cruel, coarse, or dirty person is sometimes called a *beast.*

beastly

Since the word *beast* is generally intended to convey a rather coarse image of an animal, the adjective *beastly* is used to mean unpleasant or disagreeable, as in *"beastly* weather."

bestial

Bestial is an adjective that goes back to Latin *bestia* ("beast") and means resembling a beast, lacking reason, or brutal. The word often implies a moral degradation. *Bestiality* is the noun form and means literally the condition of a lower animal and figuratively the human display of bestial traits.

Beaver

The Modern English word *beaver* for a type of rodent goes back to Old English *beofor* ("beaver"), which is based on an Indo-European root meaning "very brown." Therefore, the beaver, like the bear, is named for its brown color.

eager beaver

The beaver has a reputation for always being busy at work, mostly chewing down logs and building dams. To work hard, then, has long been known as *to work like a beaver.* But in recent years, a new expression has been coined to refer especially to someone who works hard merely for the sake of getting favors or special treatment: *eager beaver.*

work like a beaver

(See *eager beaver* above.)

Bee

The Modern English word *bee* for a type of insect goes back to Old English *beo* ("bee"), which is based on an Indo-European root meaning "bee," which may be related to a root meaning "to fear" in the sense of "to quiver," the root being applied to the bee because the insect seems to quiver while buzzing.

bee

In some parts of England, there was formerly a custom of giving voluntary help to neighbors for accomplishing particular tasks. Such help was called, in dialectal English, a *been* or *bean*, which are variants of *boon* and probably come directly from Middle English *bene* ("boon, prayer"), which comes from Old English *ben* ("prayer").

The custom was transferred to America, where, however, the name has always been recorded as *bee*, perhaps by folk etymology (influenced by the name of the insect) from dialectal English *been*. Bees have long been known for their ability to work together to fill up the community hive. And on the rough American frontier, people had good reason to take a lesson from the bees by having many community social gatherings to do special tasks. Some of the more pleasant American *bees* were "quilting *bees*," "sewing *bees*," "apple *bees*," and "husking *bees*." But there were also "shooting *bees*," "hanging *bees*," and "lynching *bees*." The most familiar *bees* today are "spelling *bees*."

beehive

A beehive is a place where bees live. It is naturally a crowded, busy place. A place where human activity is crowded and busy can also be called a *beehive*.

beeline

Folk belief has it that a bee flies in a straight line, especially when it is heading for its hive. It has become common, then, to call any direct route a *beeline*.

the birds and the bees

Parents and schools often teach children about sex by talking mostly about animal reproduction rather than human reproduction. Thus, it has become common to refer to sex itself as *the birds and the bees*.

busy as a bee

As mentioned (see *bee* and *beehive* above), the bee is noted for its apparently constant activity. To be extremely active is to be *(as) busy as a bee*.

have a bee in one's bonnet

The shape of a beehive suggests a human head. And when bees buzz in or around the hive, they make a monotonous droning sound, suggesting the monotony of a single-minded purpose. Therefore, among humans, it long ago became common to say that to be obsessed with one idea or to have fanciful or crazy ideas was *to have bees in the head* (or *brain*). Later the expression was softened and alliterated to the modern version: *to have a bee in one's bonnet*.

put the bee on

To put the bee on means to quash or to ask for a loan. It is a milder form of the expression *to put the bite on*. Both phrases originated in early twentieth-century America and may have been influenced by the earlier slang verb *to sting*, to cheat or overcharge.

Beef

The English word *beef* for bovine flesh goes back through Old French *boef* ("beef") to Latin *bov-*, which is the stem of *bos* ("ox"), which is based on an Indo-European root meaning "ox, bull, cow."

beef

Extended from its application to cattle, *beef* has come to refer to human flesh as well. Further extended, *beef* means strength. A protest, a complaint, or an argument (because of the harsh sounds from a herd of hungry cattle) is a *beef*.

beef up

Cattle are generally fattened prior to slaughter. Thus, to increase or strengthen (anything) is *to beef* (it) *up*.

Beetle

The Modern English word *beetle* for a type of insect goes back to Old English *bitela* ("beetle"), which comes from the verb *bitan* ("to bite"), which is based on an Indo-European root meaning "to split." The beetle is literally "the little biter."

beetlebrain, beetlehead

A contemptuous name for someone thought to be stupid is *beetlebrain* or *beetlehead*.

beetle-browed

Some kinds of beetles have short, tufted antennae sticking out at right angles from their heads. Some humans have heavy, projecting eyebrows that look like the beetles' antennae. People with such eyebrows are said to be *beetle-browed*.

A person who gives an angry or gloomy frown often seems to bunch up his eyebrows and push them forward. Therefore, this person is also said to be *beetle-browed*.

Behemoth

In Job 40:15-24 is described a huge animal (possibly the hippopotamus). The English word for that creature is *behemoth*, which is adopted from Hebrew *behemoth* ("great beast"), an intensive plural of *behemah* ("beast"), which may come from Egyptian *p-ehe-mau* ("water-ox").

behemoth

Anything of enormous size or power can be called, because of the large animal mentioned in Job, a *behemoth*.

Bill

The Modern English word *bill* for the beak of a bird goes back to Old English *bile* ("bill"), which is based on an Indo-European root meaning "to strike." A bird's bill, then, is "that which strikes (pecks)."

bill

Any beaklike object, such as the visor of a cap or a projection of land, can be called a *bill*.

bill and coo

Centuries ago, when birds, especially doves, stroked beak with beak, they were said to bill. That idea was applied to humans, and when people caressed or made a show of affection, they were also said *to bill*. Later the doves' cooing sound was added to the expression, so that today to be affectionate and whisper endearments is *to bill and coo*.

Bird

The Modern English word *bird* for any feathered vertebrate goes back to Old English *brid*. At first, though, *brid/bird* was applied only to a young feathered animal, while an adult was called a fowl. No one is certain where *brid* comes from, though it may be related to Old English *bredan* ("to cherish" or "to keep warm"). The original idea, then, may be that baby birds are "those protected and kept warm" by the adult fowls.

bird

An old poetic word for "woman" or "lady" was *burd*, which was not at all related to the young feathered animal *bird*. But the two words were confused so often that they finally merged into the idea of referring endearingly to a girl or young woman as a *bird*.

A man, too, can be called a *bird*, but the idea is usually lighthearted rather than endearing.

birdbrain

Birds are known to dart about aimlessly, without any real plan of action. Therefore, a person who is scatterbrained or aimless is often called a *birdbrain*.

Birds also have a reputation for having small brains. Therefore, a stupid person (that is, one with a small brain) is called a *birdbrain*.

bird dog, bird-dog

A bird dog is a dog trained to hunt or retrieve birds. Therefore, among humans, one who seeks out (such as a canvasser, a sports talent scout, or a detective) is a *bird dog*. To watch or follow closely is *to bird-dog*.

birdie

In golf, a score of one stroke less than par for a hole is called a *birdie*. The origin of the term is uncertain, but there are at least two good possibilities. One is that it evolved from the much earlier American slang use of the word *bird* to mean a person of particular quality or excellence. The other possibility is that the word simply refers to a well-hit ball that flies (according to an early, 1911, quotation) like "a 'bird' straight down the course." (Compare *eagle* under "Eagle.")

a bird in the hand is worth two in the bush

For hundreds of years, people in many languages have expressed the idea that it is better to enjoy what one has than to worry or dream about something that may be impossible to attain. In English, the most common way of saying this has become *a bird in the hand* (or *a bird in hand*) *is worth two in the bush*.

birdlime

Birdlime is a sticky substance spread on twigs to snare small birds. Figuratively, anything that ensnares is *birdlime*, as in "a *birdlime* of words."

birdman, birdwoman

An aviator is sometimes called a *birdman;* an aviatrix, a *birdwoman*.

bird of ill omen

Certain birds—notably ravens, crows, and owls—have long been regarded in folklore as bearers of bad luck. That idea has been transferred to humans, so that a person who is unlucky or who always seems to bring bad news is called a *bird of ill omen*.

bird of passage

A bird of passage is a migratory bird. Figuratively, a person who leads a wandering life is a *bird of passage*.

the birds and the bees

(See *the birds and the bees* under "Bee.")

bird's-eye

When something is seen from above, as if by a flying bird, the sight is said to be a *bird's-eye* view.

birds of a feather flock together

The expression *birds of a feather* means birds of the same type. Likewise, humans with similar interests, opinions, or backgrounds are called *birds of a feather*. And as birds of the same species tend to fly together, so, too, people with similar ideas tend to group together. Therefore, with humans as with our feathered friends, *birds of a feather flock together*.

early bird

Many birds begin to stir and sing most noticeably at the first sight of daylight in the morning. Therefore, a person who gets up or arrives early is called an *early bird*. And since a person who starts early will probably have the best chance to succeed, it is also said that *the early bird catches the worm* (that is, becomes successful).

eat like a bird

It is a traditional belief that birds, because of their typically small size, do not eat much. Therefore, a human who eats little is said *to eat like a bird*. The truth, however, is that birds eat more in relation to their size than humans do.

for the birds

Unwanted food is often tossed to birds. Therefore, anything not taken seriously is *for the birds*.

free as a bird

Wild birds do not have to worry about land obstructions; they fly where they please and when they please. Therefore, among humans, to be free in any sense, such as to be able to go anywhere or to date anyone or to take part in any activity, is to be *(as) free as a bird*.

get the bird, give the bird

In theater slang of the early 1800s, the hissing of disapproval by an audience was called *the goose* (because of the hissing noise of the animal), so that to be hissed on stage was *to get the goose.*

The goose was also called *the big bird*, usually in the expression *to get the (big) bird* (said of performers). In modern American slang, *the bird* (hissing) has developed an extended meaning, synonymous with *raspberry* and *Bronx cheer:* a jeering sound produced by placing the tongue between the two lips and blowing air.

Today, then, to be hissed or jeered (especially by an audience) or, by extension, to be dismissed from employment is *to get the bird.* In the active voice, the expression is *to give the bird.*

kill two birds with one stone

To achieve two goals with a single effort is *to kill two birds with one* (or *a single*) *stone.*

a little bird told me

In the ancient world, birds were revered for their powers of flight and vision. Many Greek and Roman soothsayers claimed birds as their sources of information. And in the Bible (Ecclesiastes 10:20) there is the following passage: " . . . a bird of the air shall carry the voice, and that which hath wings shall tell the matter." The idea of a bird carrying messages was picked up in later years, so that today when a person wants to keep secret, or to claim intuition as, a source of information he says *a little bird told me.*

Bitch

The Modern English word *bitch* for a female dog goes back to Old English *bicce* ("bitch"), which is of uncertain origin but is related to Old Norse *bikkja* ("bitch") and may go back to Latin *bestia* ("beast").

bitch

The word *bitch* was first applied only to a female dog. Now a woman who is unpleasant, selfish, malicious, or lewd is also called a *bitch*.

From the noun has come a verb: to complain is *to bitch*.

Bloodsucker

A bloodsucker is any animal that sucks blood, especially the leach. The name comes simply from combining *blood* and *sucker*.

bloodsucker

A bloodsucker lives by preying on the blood of other animals. Among humans, then, one who preys on another's money or property is said to be a *bloodsucker*.

Booby

The English word *booby* for a type of seabird comes from Spanish *bobo* ("fool"), which goes back to Latin *balbus* ("stammering"), which is based on an Indo-European root imitative of a stammer. The bird is so named because of its comical awkwardness on its feet.

booby hatch

A certain hatch on a ship is called a *booby hatch* because it is a favorite resting place for boobies, the seabirds. From the nautical sense, *booby hatch* has extended to mean a jail or any kind of lockup. A *booby hatch* is also an insane asylum or a place suggesting an insane asylum (some authorities say because of the crazy antics of the boobies on a ship, others say because of the influence of the word *booby* meaning fool—probably the senses of bird and fool conjoin here).

Brute

The English word *brute* for an animal goes back to Latin *brutus* ("stupid" or "heavy"), which is based on an Indo-European root meaning "heavy."

brute, brutal, brutish

A male human being who is cruel, crude, and lacking in intelligence is sometimes called a *brute*.

Brute as an adjective means inhuman, irrational, cruel, or simply characteristic of the fundamental powers in all creatures, as in *"brute* instinct" and *"brute* strength."

Brutal means cruel. *Brutish* usually applies to manners and means lacking in human refinement.

Buck

The Modern English word *buck* for a male animal (especially a deer or an antelope) goes back to Old English *buc* ("male deer") and *bucca* ("he-goat"), which are based on an Indo-European root meaning "male animal (stag, ram, he-goat)." Some authorities suggest that *buck* may be borrowed from a Celtic form (as represented in Old Irish *bocc,* "he-goat") and that the Celtic word means "the beast that flees."

buck

A male human being, especially one who is young or impetuous or foppish, is sometimes called a *buck*.

In the early days on the American frontier, buckskins were often the main units for trading. Later the dollar replaced the buckskin but kept the word *buck* as a nickname.

When an animal, especially a horse, leaps into the air to dislodge a rider or a pack from its back, the animal, because of the similarity of its actions to those of a frisky male deer, is said *to buck.* Among humans, then, to refuse assent is *to buck.* And when a person tries to resist or object to something, he is (like the horse attempting to dislodge the rider) trying *to buck* it.

buck for

As the bucking horse attempts to win something (its freedom), so a person who struggles for something (such as a promotion) is said *to buck for* it.

bucktooth

A large projecting front tooth is called a *bucktooth*.

pass the buck

The expression *to pass the buck* comes from the card game poker as it was played in nineteenth-century America. An object was placed into the pot to remind a player that he had to perform some duty (such as to deal). This object was called a *buck* because it was originally a knife with a buck-horn handle. To pass the buck to another player was to shift the responsibility of performing the duty. Today to avoid any responsibility or blame by passing it to another person is *to pass the buck*.

sawbuck

A frame for holding wood being cut is called a *sawbuck* (from Dutch *zaagbok*, "sawbuck") or a *sawhorse* (see *sawhorse* under "Horse"). The name comes from the fact that the frame brings to mind the general shape of a buck or a horse.

Such a frame often consists of one or more X-shaped sections. Since X is the Roman numeral for ten, and since a dollar is known as a *buck*, a ten-dollar bill has come to be called a *sawbuck*.

Buffalo

The English word *buffalo* for a type of wild oxen goes back to Greek *boubalos* (originally "African antelope," later "buffalo"), a derivative of Greek *bous* ("ox, bull, cow"), which is based on an Indo-European root meaning "ox, bull, cow."

The American animal commonly known as a buffalo is not a true buffalo, such as the buffalo of Africa and Asia. The American type is actually a bison.

buff

A thick oil-tanned leather made of buffalo skin is called buff. Real buff leather has become rare, but now leather made of other animal skins is also known as *buff*. Since buff is often used to brighten up metal, it is commonly said that to shine or polish something is *to buff* it (even though buff leather itself is not used).

The light yellow or tan of buff leather is said to resemble the color of some types of human skin. Therefore, the bare skin of humans is sometimes called the *buff*, as in "strip to the *buff*" and "in the *buff*."

New York City volunteer firemen used to wear buff uniforms. From that fact came the practice of referring to all people who liked to go to fires as *buffs*. Today an enthusiast or fan of any subject or activity is known as a *buff*, as in "film *buff*" and "sports *buff*."

buffalo

On the American frontier, the buffalo (that is, the bison) was noted for being powerful and ornery. Therefore, it is said that to frighten or confuse someone is *to buffalo* him.

Bug

The origin of the word *bug* for an insect is uncertain. But *bug* is usually assumed to be a transferred use of Middle English *bugge* ("bugbear, scarecrow"), which probably comes from Welsh *bug* ("ghost, hobgoblin"). A bug, then, would be named for its grotesque appearance.

bug

A prominent person or one of assumed importance is called a *bug*, often "big *bug*." According to the *Oxford English Dictionary*, this sense of the word was originally an extension of *bug* meaning bugbear (or perhaps of an obsolete adjective *bug* meaning pompous, big, proud) but is now regarded by those who use it as referring to *bug* meaning insect.

An enthusiast or a hobbyist is called a *bug*, as in "baseball *bug*." And one having an obsessive idea is a *bug*, as in "litterbug" and "firebug." The obsession itself is also a *bug*. Standard authorities do not explain why *bug* is used in this sense, but the word is usually listed in dictionaries under *bug* meaning insect. The reference is probably to a bug's apparent obsession to accomplish a task, as in the expression *(as) crazy as a bedbug* (see *crazy as a bedbug* below), which originated at about the same time (the early 1800s) as *bug* meaning enthusiast.

A defect in a system is called a *bug*. The reference here is to an imaginary mischievous entity (combining the senses of "invisible" bugbear and "tiny" insect) that secretly causes problems. This sense was recorded in 1889 in a reference to a *bug* in Thomas Edison's phonograph.

A disease-producing microorganism is called a *bug* because, like an insect, a microbe is tiny and often has a weird shape. An infection resulting from the effects of a microbe is also a *bug*, as in "flu *bug*." These senses were first recorded in the early 1900s.

At one time, any automobile was called a *bug* because early car owners were thought to be *bugs* in the sense of enthusiasts. Later *bug* referred to any small car because of its size, and especially today to the Volkswagen because of its buglike shape.

A concealed listening device is called a *bug*. This sense of the word has been used since the late 1940s. Some authorities say that the word refers to the small, buglike appearance of early types of such devices. Others say that the word comes from the cardsharper's *bug* (recorded since the late 1800s), a device that is hidden under the table and used to hold cards for cheating. The cardsharper's *bug* in turn is probably named for its image of buglike concealment and small size. Or the cardsharper's *bug* may be an extension of an earlier *bug* meaning tiepin, since the cardsharper's device typically consists of a spring, like that on a tiepin. In turn, *bug* meaning tiepin is probably named for its small, buglike size and shininess. In any case, *bug* meaning concealed listening device eventually goes back to the insect. (However, a possible noninsect influence is the *bug* that is short for *burglar alarm*; this *bug* is recorded since the 1920s.)

A weight allowance given apprentice jockeys is called a *bug* because of the buglike asterisk that designates the handicap on race programs.

To equip with a concealed listening device or to annoy (both senses since the 1940s) is *to bug*.

bug-eyed

Since most insects seem to have fixed, protruding eyes, a person whose eyes are bulging from surprise is described as being *bug-eyed*.

buggy

Buggy, in its original sense, means infested with bugs. Because of the creepy image it brings to mind, in American slang the word has come to mean crazy (as if bugs were crawling in the head).

bughouse

Bug meaning one obsessed with an idea yields *bughouse*, which as a noun means insane asylum and as an adjective means crazy.

bugs

Bugs, like *buggy* (see *buggy* above), is a reference to the fanciful image of bugs crawling in the head and means crazy.

crazy as a bedbug

Bedbugs are small insects that hide during the day and then feed on human, or other animal, blood at night. Bedbugs are smart and persistent. If bedposts are put into pots of water so that the insects cannot crawl up, the bedbugs will climb to the ceiling and drop onto the bed. People sometimes refer to a mentally unstable person as being *(as) crazy as a bedbug*. This expression probably refers to the bedbug's seemingly crazed obsession with getting into a bed and sucking human blood. (See also *bug* meaning enthusiast above.)

put a bug in one's ear

To drop a little hint is *to put a bug in one's ear*.

snug as a bug in a rug

To be perfectly comfortable is to be *(as) snug as a bug in a rug*.

Bull

The Modern English word *bull* for an adult male animal (especially a bovine) goes back to Old English *bula* ("bull"), which is based on an Indo-European root meaning "to swell," which is applied to the bull in reference to the animal's reproductive function.

bear and bull

(See *bear and bull* under "Bear.")

bull

A large, solidly built man is sometimes called a *bull*.

To behave like a bull by forcing or shoving is *to bull*, as in "*to bull* one's way through the crowd."

bulldozer

A severe whipping was in the late 1800s called a *bulldose* (that is, a "big dose"), also spelled *bulldoze*, either because the dose of beating was given with a bullwhip or because the dose was harsh enough to be fit for a bull. One who administered such a whipping, or one who threatened violence in any way, was called a *bulldozer*. Later came the invention of a big, earth-moving tractor that brutally pushed aside everything in its path just as a violent person did; therefore, such a tractor was also called a *bulldozer*.

bullhorn

A high-powered handheld loudspeaker, because of its strength (recalling that of a bull), is called a *bullhorn*.

bull in a china shop

A bull in a china shop would carelessly shatter many delicate objects. And a person who does something without regard for the physical damage or the hurt feelings he causes, especially in a delicate situation, creates an impression similar to that of the clumsy bull and can therefore be called a *bull in a china shop*. The origin of this expression might be related to an old fable in which an ass, pictured as clumsy and stupid, breaks most of the earthen pots in a potter's shop; that idea could then have been transferred to the bull. Another theory is that the expression comes from a political event: in the early nineteenth century, a man was sent from England (nicknamed John Bull, as the United States is nicknamed Uncle Sam) to foster trade with China, but the

Englishman (the Bull) failed and therefore shattered everyone's hopes for success on his delicate China mission.

bullpen

A bullpen is a place to keep a bull, especially just before the animal is sent into the ring for a bullfight. A cell for prisoners, because of its shape, has also come to be known as a *bullpen*. Today the term is heard most often in baseball: the (usually) enclosed place where relief pitchers warm up is called a *bullpen*, probably because of its shape, though some have said that the name comes from the early days of baseball when the warm-up area was often under a billboard ad of Bull Durham tobacco.

bull's-eye

The term *bull's-eye* has been applied to many kinds of circular objects, most commonly today to the center of a target. The shot that hits the center is also called a *bull's-eye*. Figuratively, anything that precisely attains a desired end is a *bull's-eye*.

bullwhip

A certain kind of rawhide whip with a long plaited lash is called a *bullwhip*. It is so named for any one of three reasons: it is large and heavy (like a bull); it was, in the early days, often made from a bull's body; and it was, in the Old West, used to drive teams of male bovines.

cock-and-bull story

Stories in which animals talk and act like humans have been told since mankind's earliest recorded tales. But practical people have always referred to the stories as being unrealistic. Any unbelievable story, with or without animal characters, has in the French language long been known as a *coq-à-l'âne* ("cock-to-the-donkey") story. In English, the expression has become *cock-and-bull story*.

take the bull by the horns

In both bulldogging and bullfighting, one must grab a strong animal by the horns—in bulldogging, to take a steer to the ground; in bullfighting, to put on a show (in Portuguese style) with a bull or to protect oneself when a bull is about to toss one. Clearly this operation must be done quickly and fearlessly. Therefore, to attack any difficult task with courage is *to take the bull by the horns.*

Bulldog

The word *bulldog* for a type of canine comes either from the animal's use in bullbaiting or from the bull-like shape of its head.

bulldog

The bulldog is known for its courageous and obstinate fighting. A courageous, tenacious person is sometimes called a *bulldog.*

To attack or fight with the bulldog's characteristics is *to bulldog.* Out of that idea comes a specific use in the American West of the verb *to bulldog:* to throw a steer (or other animal) to the ground by grabbing its horns and twisting its neck is *to bulldog* the animal.

Bun

Bun is a Scottish and northern (England) dialectal word meaning "tail of a hare." It probably comes from Gaelic *bun* ("root, stump, bottom").

bun

A human posterior is sometimes called a *bun.*

Bunny

The Modern English word *bunny* for a rabbit (especially a young rabbit) is a diminutive of the earlier English dialectal word *bun* ("rabbit"), which is believed to be an extension of Scottish and northern (England) dialectal *bun* ("tail of a hare"), which probably comes from Gaelic *bun* ("root, stump, bottom").

bunny

Bunny is a term of endearment, especially for a woman or a child. It is also a nickname for *Roberta* or *Barbara*.

In slang use, *bunny* is any person, as in "tough *bunny*." More often, it implies a mild, even affectionate, criticism of a person who is somewhat confused or foolish, as in "dumb *bunny*" and "helpless *bunny*."

bunny hop

In figure skating, a short leap to gain speed is a *bunny hop*. In snow skiing, a dip in a ski trail is a *bunny hop*.

Butterfly

The word *butterfly* for a type of insect is formed from *butter* and *fly* ("fly," the insect; see "Fly"). The reason for the name is unknown. A Dutch synonym suggests that the insect is so named because of the appearance of its excrement. But some authorities say that the name simply refers to the yellow color of the most common varieties. Others say that the name may come from the belief that butterflies or witches in the shape of butterflies steal milk and butter.

butterflies (in the stomach)

Fluttering sensations caused by nervous anticipation are called, in reference to the movements of the insect, *butterflies (in the stomach)*.

butterfly

The butterfly is noted for its bouncy, darting movements in quickly changing directions. Therefore, a person who flits aimlessly from one idea or group to another is called a *butterfly*, as in "social *butterfly*."

butterfly stroke

A swimming stroke in which both arms move in a circular motion while the legs kick up and down simultaneously is called, in reference to the insect's wing movement, a *butterfly stroke*. (See also *dolphin kick* under "Dolphin.")

butterfly table

A table having leaves (sides) that can go up or down is called, because of the winglike action of the leaves, a *butterfly table.*

Buzzard

The English word *buzzard* for a type of bird goes back to Old French *busard* ("buzzard"), which goes back to Latin *buteo* ("a kind of hawk"), which is based on an Indo-European root imitative of muffled sounds. *Buteo* is related to Latin *butire* ("to cry like a bitern," literally "to utter the sound *bu*"). The buzzard therefore owes its name to the *bu* sound that the ancient Romans associated with certain birds.

buzzard

Formerly, an important sport in England was falconry (hunting with trained hawks). The buzzard was rated as an inferior sort of hawk, useless for falconry. Therefore, any worthless, stupid person came to be called a *buzzard.* Today a disliked person, especially an old man with a streak of meanness, is called a *buzzard,* often an "old *buzzard.*"

say turkey to (one) and buzzard to (another)

(See *talk turkey, say turkey to (one) and buzzard to (another)* under "Turkey.")

Calf

The Modern English word *calf* for a young animal goes back to Old English *cealf* ("calf"), which is based on an Indo-European root meaning "to swell out" and its extensions meaning "swelling, fetus, offspring."

calf

A calf is the young of the domestic cow or of a closely related mammal. In reference to the typical clumsiness of the young animal, an awkward, silly boy or young man is often called a *calf.*

calf-eyes

Flirting eyes or other forms of flirtatious conduct are known as *calf-eyes.*

calf love

The temporary infatuation of a boy and a girl is known as *calf love.* (See also *puppy love* under "Puppy.")

kill the fatted calf

In the biblical account of the rejoicing at the return of the prodigal son occurs this line (Luke 15:23): "And bring hither the fatted calf, and kill it; and let us eat, and be merry." Today to prepare an elaborate welcome (with or without serving calf meat) is *to kill the fatted calf.*

Camel

The English word *camel* for a humped desert ruminant goes back to Latin *camelus* ("camel"), which comes from Greek *kamelos* ("camel"), which derives from Hebrew and Phoenician *gamal* ("camel") or Arabic *jamal* ("camel") or Egyptian *kamal* ("camel"). The origin of the word may lie in a Semitic verb (as in Arabic *jamala*) meaning "to bear," the camel being a beast of burden.

camel

In technology, a *camel* is a structure filled with water (like the hump of a camel), attached to a submerged ship, and pumped out so that it will rise and pull up the ship with it.

A variable color averaging light yellowish brown (like the animal's color) is called *camel.*

strain at a gnat and swallow a camel

In the Bible (Matthew 23:24) occurs this line: "Ye blind guides, which strain at a gnat, and swallow a camel." Here the small gnat is metaphorically any trifle, while the large camel is any serious matter. Today, then, to fuss about unimportant issues while assenting too readily in important ones is *to strain at a gnat and swallow a camel.*

the straw that broke the camel's back

There are a great many phrases in various languages expressing the idea that a small thing, if culminating a series of small things, can cause a big effect. Seneca, in ancient Rome, wrote: "It is not the last drop that empties the waterclock, but all that has previously flowed out." Francis Bacon, in early seventeeth-century England, wrote: "As the Spanish Proverb noteth well: The cord breaketh at the last by the weakest pull." Archbishop John Bramhall, in late seventeenth-century England, wrote: "It is the last feather that breaks the horse's back."

By the nineteenth century, the phrase had become *the straw that broke the camel's back.* The camel is noted as a durable beast of burden. Thus, it is a useful symbol for anything that is strong but that has a limit, which is finally reached by the "last straw."

Canary

The word *canary* for a type of bird comes from the name of the Canary Islands, a group of islands off the west coast of Africa. *Canary* goes back through French and Spanish forms to Latin *Canaria insula* ("Dog Island" or "Island of Dogs"), which is based on Latin *canis* ("dog") because of the large dogs reportedly found there.

canary

The canary bird is so named because it was found on the Canary Islands. In turn, the yellow color of the canary bird has become known as the *canary* color. Since the bird is noted for its singing, a human singer (especially a female) is known as a *canary*. A criminal who informs on his accomplices (that is, "sings" to the police) is also a *canary*.

look like the cat that swallowed the canary

To look self-satisfied is *to look like the cat that swallowed the canary.*

Cat

The English word *cat* for a type of mammal goes back to Late Latin *cattus* ("cat"), which may come from an African language (Nubian, for example, has *kadis*, "cat").

alley cat

A stray cat is commonly called an alley cat. Extended, *alley cat*, in slang, means a prostitute or any person sexually loose. (See also *cat* and *cathouse* below.)

bell the cat

There is a fable, told in many different versions, about a group of mice (or rats) that had been troubled by a cat. The mice held a meeting and decided that they could tell where the cat was at all times if they simply put a bell around the cat's neck. They were all pleased with their decision until one farsighted mouse spoke up and said that the idea was fine, but *who* would bell the cat? Today, among humans, to attempt anything dangerous, especially for the benefit of others, is *to bell the cat*.

cat

Since medieval times, the superstitious have believed that Satan often takes the form of a black cat. Witches are also associated with cats. Because of those beliefs and because of the cat's habit of scratching people, an evil-minded gossipy woman (who "scratches" others with her words) is often called a *cat*.

In slang, a *cat* is a prostitute (see also *alley cat* above and *cathouse* below), a jazz expert, and a man (especially a "regular guy," one of the group).

cat-and-dog

Since cats and dogs are well known for their fights, they are often verbally put together to describe something that is wild and destructive, such as a *"cat-and-dog* competition."

cat burglar

Cats are known for their climbing ability. A burglar who

enters a home by some extraordinary feat of climbing, such as going through an upstairs window, is called a *cat burglar*.

catcall

Another cat characteristic is the screeching cry it sometimes makes. In England, a *catcall* was a small whistle that produced a sound like the cry of a cat and was formerly used in theaters to express disapproval. Today any similar sound, especially one made at a theater to express disapproval of the performance, is known as a *catcall*.

caterwaul

It is said of cats that to make their characteristic noises during rutting time is to caterwaul. Extended to humans, *to caterwaul* means to make any harsh cry or to quarrel noisily.

cat-eyed

To have eyes resembling those of a cat, or to be capable (like a cat) of seeing in dark places, is to be *cat-eyed*.

catfacing

In fruit, a disfigurement or malformation suggesting a cat's face in appearance (such as that caused on the surface of a tomato by an improper water balance) is called *catfacing*.

cat has got one's tongue

When one cannot speak, especially from surprise or fear, the *cat has got one's tongue*.

cathouse

A *cat* being a prostitute (see *alley cat* and *cat* above), a brothel is a *cathouse*.

a cat may look at a king

A cat may look at a king means that even an "inferior" has certain rights in the presence of a "superior."

catnap

Cats have a habit of dozing off for brief periods of time. Therefore, a short, light nap for a person is called a *catnap*.

cat on a hot tin roof

In England, *hot bricks* is an old expression denoting a situation of extreme discomfort and restlessness, especially in the phrase *like a cat on hot bricks*. In 1955, the American writer Tennessee Williams won a Pulitzer Prize for his play *Cat on a Hot Tin Roof,* so that now, in America at least, a restless person is said to be a *cat on a hot tin roof.*

cat-o'-nine-tails

A *cat-o'-nine-tails* is a whip, usually having nine knotted lines or cords fastened to a handle. It was formerly used for administering punishment to seamen aboard ships. Popular superstition said that nine knots (or "tails") were used because a flogging by a "trinity of trinities" would have symbolic significance. The victim of the beating was left with scars that looked like cat scratches. Thus, the whip was nicknamed a *cat* of nine tails.

cat's-eye

Anything resembling the eye of a cat is called a *cat's-eye,* such as any of various gems or a kind of child's marble.

cat's-paw

There is a fable about a monkey that used the paw of a cat (in older versions, a dog) to scrape chestnuts out of a fire. The cat's paw, of course, got burned. Today a person who is easily tricked into doing something dangerous or foolish for someone else is called a *cat's-paw.* (See also *pull chestnuts out of the fire* under "Animal-related Expressions" in Part Two.)

catty

To resemble a cat, especially in its sneaky or lightfooted manner, is to be *catty.* More specifically, a person who is hatefully sly and mean (supposedly like a cat) is known as a *catty* person.

catwalk

The cat is noted for being able to walk along extremely

narrow paths. Therefore, any narrow walkway can be called a *catwalk*.

copycat

An imitator is called a *copycat*. The origin of this expression is uncertain, but it is probably due partly to characteristics of the animal and partly to alliteration.

curiosity killed the cat

It is proverbially said that a cat has nine lives (see *have as many lives as a cat* below); that is, it can survive many scrapes. Since at least the 1500s, people have used the expression *care killed the cat* to mean that care (worry) would finally kill anyone, even though he, like the cat, had nine lives to spend. *Care* refers to the cat's careful behavior, and it alliterates with *killed* and *cat*. Eventually the expression changed to *curiosity killed the cat*, partly because of the influence of earlier expressions about harm coming to the curious. For example, Saint Augustine, in his *Confessions*, quoted an unnamed author who made the following reply when asked what God was doing before He made heaven and earth: "He fashioned hell for the inquisitive." A later author wrote: "He that pryeth into every cloud, may be struck with a thunderbolt." The word *curiosity*, then, easily slipped into the mold of *care killed the cat*. Furthermore, *curiosity* fulfills the same alliterative function as *care* does.

fat cat

In *fat cat*, *cat* is slang for any person (see *cat* above). *Fat* means bloated with money. A *fat cat* is a wealthy person, especially one who helps finance a political campaign.

have as many lives as a cat

Because the cat seems to be so careful and always seems to land on its feet without an injury (see *land on one's feet* under "Animal-related Expressions" in Part Two), folklore has it that the cat has nine lives. That idea can be traced back to ancient India and to fables by the reputed author Bidpai.

Nine has been a mystical number since ancient times in many societies. Pythagoreans in ancient Greece believed that man was a full "chord" of eight tones; adding the deity made nine. In Christianity, three is the trinity, or perfect unity; twice three is the perfect dual; and thrice three (nine) is the perfect plural.

Since at least the 1500s, English speakers have utilized the idea of the cat's nine lives in various expressions. In general, then, to be durable is *to have as many lives as a cat*.

holy cats

Holy cats is a euphemism for the interjection *Holy Christ*.

let the cat out of the bag

In England, people used to take young pigs to market in a poke (a bag). It was a common trick to put a cat into the bag to try to sell the worthless cat as a valuable pig. A foolish buyer would pay for the animal without even opening the bag to see if there was a cat or a pig inside. Today to buy anything without knowing its true value is *to buy a pig in a poke*. A smart buyer, of course, would insist on opening the poke. If a cat was inside, it would jump out and expose the trick. Today to reveal any secret is *to let the cat out of the bag*.

look like something the cat has brought in

A cat is often seen walking about with a small dead animal hanging limply out of its mouth. A person can be compared to the impression given by the dead animal; to look (or feel) tired or messy is *to look* (or *feel*) *like something the cat has brought* (or *dragged*) *in*.

look like the cat that swallowed the canary

(See *look like the cat that swallowed the canary* under "Canary.")

more than one way to skin a cat

In the 1800s, there were many variants of the common expression *there are more ways of killing a cat than choking her with cream*. The version that has endured is one created, or used very early, by Samuel Clemens (Mark Twain) in *A Connecticut Yankee in King Arthur's Court*: "She knew more than one way to skin a cat." Today, then, to have various available solutions is to have *more than one way to skin a cat.*

not enough room to swing a cat

To have only a small space available is to have *not enough* (or *no*) *room to swing a cat.* The origin of this expression is uncertain, though several theories have been published. The most commonly found explanation is that *cat* stands for *cat-o'-nine-tails,* the whip formerly used for punishment aboard ships. When the whip was used to flog someone, the beating had to take place on the open deck because in the cramped quarters belowdecks there was simply not enough room to swing the whip (the *cat*). However, the expression *not enough room to swing a cat* was recorded long before *cat* was recorded as short for *cat-o'-nine-tails.*

Another theory is that the expression refers to the barbarous custom of putting a cat into a bag, suspending it from a tree limb, and shooting at it with arrows for target practice. It has also been suggested that *cat* may be a sailors' corruption of *cot,* a hammock sometimes hanging (swinging) in a confined space.

The truth is that *cat* has meant so many different things that it is impossible to tell exactly which one is the original referent in the expression *not enough room to swing a cat.* For example, in the game of tipcat, *cat* was at one time short for *cat-stick,* the stick used to swing at a little piece of tapered wood. The timing of that sense (early 1600s) would have been right to influence the origin of *not enough room to swing a cat* (first recorded in the mid-1600s). But did it?

Finally it must be suggested that the original reference might very well have been quite literal. The expression originated at a time when many forms of savagery against animals, such as badgerbaiting and the above-mentioned practice of shooting at bagged cats, were common. The cat is ubiquitous (for easy access), long tailed (for easy grasping), and lightweight (for easy swinging)—a logical referent for a jocular (or as one writer in 1665 called it, "vulgar") way of expressing the measurement of space around a human pivot.

play cat and mouse with

After trapping a mouse, a cat will often toy with the poor animal before making the final strike. Among humans, to tease or torment someone, or to overpower and simply wait for the chance to destroy a person, is *to play cat and mouse with* him.

rain cats and dogs

To rain heavily is *to rain cats and dogs*. Some people think that this expression comes from Norse mythology, in which cats are symbols of rainstorms (perhaps from their scratching on roofs) and dogs are symbols of winds (perhaps from their barking "wind"). But whatever the original idea was, the reference today is simply to the fact that the thunder, lightning, wind, and rain remind one of the wild fury of a cat-and-dog fight.

scaredy-cat

Since cats are noted for their sometimes excessive cautiousness, an unduly fearful person is called a *scaredy-cat*.

see which way the cat jumps

To see which way (or *see how*) *the cat jumps* means to await the course of events before committing oneself to an opinion or a course of action. The reference is probably either to the game of tipcat (in which one must await the direction of the wood *cat* before striking it) or to the cruel pastime of hanging a cat in a bag as a target.

tomcat

In 1760 England, a book called *The Life and Adventures of a Cat* was published by an anonymous author. The hero of the story is a feline named Tom the Cat. The book was so popular that soon any male cat was called a tomcat. *Tom* also came to be applied to the male of various beasts and birds. Now a sexually active man is a *tomcat*, and (said of a male) to search for a sexual partner is *to tomcat*.

when the cat's away, the mice will play

When a cat is not nearby, mice certainly have more

freedom—often to do mischief. So, too, of a person who may get into mischief when no one is there to watch him, it is said that *when the cat's away, the mice will play.*

Catbird

A catbird is an American songbird. The word *catbird* comes from the fact that the bird's cry of alarm resembles the meow of a cat.

catbird seat

A *catbird seat* is a position of great advantage or prominence. The expression was first popularized by the baseball announcer "Red" Barber in radio broadcasts of the 1940s. James Thurber picked up the expression and wrote a famous story called "The Catbird Seat." The reason for the expression is uncertain. Barber himself is reported to have said that he got the expression from a poker pal who, after beating Barber in a game, stated that he knew that he (the pal) had a good hand and was therefore "sitting in the catbird seat."

Since the catbird is a songbird, it has been conjectured that the bird, perched high and singing contentedly, suggested to some phrase-coiner's mind a person in complete control of a situation.

However, many birds perch and sing. So why was the catbird chosen for this particular expression? Perhaps there was, in fact, no logical reason. But perhaps the word *catbird* suggested the image of a cat ready to pounce on a nearby bird. A *catbird seat*, then, would be the location (seat) where one entity (the cat) dominates another (the bird); hence, a *catbird seat* would be any position of advantage.

Caterpillar

The English word *caterpillar* for a wormlike larva goes back to Old North French *catepelose* ("caterpillar"), which is a compound of *cate* ("cat," from Late Latin *catta*) and *pelose* ("hairy," from Late Latin *pilosa*, from Latin *pilosus*, from *pilus*, "hair"). The caterpillar, then, is "the hairy cat," so named because of its hairy covering. The -*pillar* part of the English word was probably arrived at by folk etymology from Old North French -*pelose* through the influence of obsolete English *piller* ("pillager"), the caterpillar being noted for its destruction of garden plants.

caterpillar

An amusement-park device with a series of connected cars running on an undulating track is called, because of its appearance, a *caterpillar*.

caterpillar tractor

A type of tractor with two endless metal belts, one on each side of the machine, is called a *caterpillar tractor* because the belts suggest the bodies of caterpillars (from the trademark Caterpillar).

Cattle

The Modern English word *cattle* for livestock goes back through Middle English and Old North French *catel* ("personal property, livestock") to Latin *capitale* ("property") to Latin *capitalis* ("principal") to Latin *caput* ("head") to an Indo-European root meaning "head."

cattle

A contemptuous name for a mass of humans is *cattle*.

Chameleon

The English word *chameleon* for a type of lizard goes back to Greek *khamaileon* ("chameleon"), which is built from two smaller Greek words: *khamai* ("on the ground" or "dwarf") and *leon* ("lion"). The chameleon, then, is "the lion on the ground" or "the dwarf lion," so named because of the chameleon's lionlike appearance.

chameleon

The chameleon is a lizard noted especially for its ability to change the color of its skin. A person who keeps changing his opinion or attitude (as a chameleon keeps changing its color) is called a *chameleon*.

Chamois

The English word *chamois* for a type of antelope comes from French *chamois* ("chamois"), which comes from Late Latin *camox* ("chamois"), which is apparently an Alpine word of Indo-European origin but of uncertain meaning.

chamois

A type of soft, pliable leather, originally of chamois skin but now of the skin of other animals, is called *chamois*. A cotton cloth finished to simulate such leather is also a *chamois*.

A grayish yellow color, like that of the animal leather, is *chamois*.

To clean or polish with a *chamois* is *to chamois*.

Chick

Chick is short for *chicken*.

chick

A male or female child, like a young chicken, has long been referred to as a *chick*. Today, however, the most common use of the word is in reference to a young woman.

Chicken

The Modern English word *chicken* for a type of fowl goes back to Old English *cicen* ("chicken"). Some authorities say that *cicen* means literally "little cock" and is a diminutive of Old English *cocc* ("cock"), which originates as an imitation of the bird's cry. Other authorities, however, suggest that Old English *cicen* is based on an Indo-European root meaning "a hollow place, a round object, a lump," a reference to the chicken's laying of eggs.

chicken

Chickens are easily frightened. A coward is often called a *chicken*.

chicken feed

Chickens are commonly tossed food too poor in quality for human use. Low-quality food suggests low-value money. Hence, insignificant amounts of money are called *chicken feed*.

chickenhearted, chicken-livered

In England, the heart is traditionally the seat of courage (as in Richard the Lionhearted). Therefore, to be cowardly is to be *chickenhearted*. (See *chicken* above.)

But in the Romance languages the heart is traditionally the seat of love, while the liver is the seat of courage (as in the Italian expression *un uomo pieno di fegato*, "a man with plenty of liver," that is, "guts"). Therefore, to be cowardly is to be *chicken-livered*. (See *chicken* above.)

chicken out

To avoid doing something because of fear is *to chicken out*. (See *chicken* above.)

chickens always come home to roost

It was once commonly said (with many variants) that *curses, like chickens, always come home to roost*. It was a barnyard way of expressing the biblical "Judge not, that ye be not judged" (Matthew 7:1)—that is, a person's harsh judgments (curses) of other people may one day be used against him (return to him like chickens returning to their roost). Today that idea has broadened: to say that a person's wrong actions of any kind will return to haunt him in the future is to say that his *chickens always come home to roost*.

count one's chickens before they are hatched

Since some eggs in a particular group may not hatch properly, it would be unwise to plan one's future (such as a farmer's legally committing himself to some sort of purchase) on the assumption that all of the eggs will produce healthy chickens. Related to that idea is a fable in which a woman was going to market with a basket full of eggs. As she walked, she planned her future. She would sell the eggs to buy a goose. Then she would fatten the goose, sell it, and buy a cow. But while she was planning, she dropped the basket, smashing the eggs. Today to rely on something that is still uncertain is *to count one's chickens before they are hatched.*

run around like a chicken with its head cut off

If the head of a live chicken is cut off, the animal will flop about wildly for some time. Therefore, to be wildly busy is *to run around like a chicken with its head cut off.*

spring chicken

In the days before incubators, farmers found that the chickens hatched in early spring brought the best prices. Sometimes farmers tried to deceive customers into buying an old chicken as part of the spring crop. But smart buyers would examine the tough old bird and say that it was no spring chicken. Today any young person can be called a *spring chicken.*

up with the chickens

Since the rooster is known for its early morning crowing, chickens are traditionally thought of as being early risers. Therefore, to be up early is to be *up with the chickens.*

Chit

The English word *chit* formerly meant "kitten, cub, whelp." *Chit* may be a thinning of Old French *chat* ("cat") and be influenced in meaning by *kitten.*

chit

A child or a pert young woman is a *chit.*

Chub

The origin of the word *chub* for a type of fish is uncertain. But *chub* may be related to some Scandinavian words (such as Swedish dialectal *kubb*) that mean "log of wood" and are based on an Indo-European root meaning "a hollow place, a round object, a lump." The chub fish, then, is probably so named in reference to its thick, fat body.

chubby

Because of the chub's fat appearance, a person who is plump and well rounded is called *chubby*.

Clam

The Modern English word *clam* for a type of bivalve shellfish is shortened from *clamshell*, which comes from Old English *clamm* ("clamp"), which is based on an Indo-European root meaning "to make round, clench." The clam, then, is named for the clamping action of the animal's shells.

clam

Since the two shells of the clam suggest the appearance of the human mouth, the mouth is sometimes called a *clam*.

The most obvious characteristic of the clam is the way it can quickly and tightly close its two valves, or shells. Therefore, a closemouthed person is called a *clam*, and to stop talking is *to clam up*.

Some American Indians used clams for money. Today a dollar is sometimes called a *clam*.

clambake

A clambake is a traditional seaside picnic at which the baking of clams is the main event. Now any social gathering, especially an informal, noisy one, is called a *clambake*.

clam up

(See *clam* above.)

happy as a clam

Along the Atlantic coast tidal flats of the United States, soft-shell clams lie buried in the sand. Clams have two reasons for being happy at high tide. One is that they feed when the water is up. The other is that high tide protects them from humans who dig up the clams during low tide.

People living near the seashore have developed an expression relating to clams: to be in good spirits is to be *(as) happy as a clam at high tide* (or *water*), usually shortened to *(as) happy as a clam.*

Cobweb

The Modern English word *cobweb* for a spider's network comes from Middle English *coppeweb*, which is a combination of *coppe* ("spider," shortened from Old English *atorcoppe*, literally "poison head") and *web* ("web," based on the same root as Middle English *weven* and Old English *wefan*, "to weave"). The cobweb, then, is "the spider-woven thing."

cobweb

Since a spider's web is a lightweight structure, anything flimsy can be called a *cobweb*.

The web, of course, traps insects. Therefore, any plan to trap someone or something can be called a *cobweb*.

cobwebs

Since cobwebs tend to blur the appearance of the area in which they are located, any kind of confusion or lack of order can be called *cobwebs*, as when a person says, "My head is filled with *cobwebs*."

Cock

The Modern English word *cock* for a rooster goes back to Old English *cocc* ("cock") and is originally an attempt to imitate the cry of the animal. Old English *cocc* is probably influenced in form by Latin *coco* ("cackle").

cock

Because a cock, or rooster, typically dominates the hens, any leader can be called a *cock*.

Cock also stands for a faucet that controls the flow of a liquid. The name probably comes from the faucet's shape looking somewhat like the animal's head and comb.

Because of its original shape, the hammer that causes

the discharge in a firearm is known as a *cock*. And to pull the hammer back into place for firing is *to cock* it.

Probably in reference to the animal's outstretched crest or tail or neck in crowing come many uses of the verb *to cock* meaning in general to set, turn, tip, or tilt up or to one side, as in "He likes *to cock* (turn up) his hat brim," "He *cocked* (tilted) his hat to the left side of his head," "The dog *cocked* his ears at the sound," and "She relaxed by *cocking* her feet up on the desk."

cock-and-bull story

(See *cock-and-bull story* under "Bull.")

cockeyed

As mentioned (see *cock* above), the word *cock* can mean turned to one side. Literally, then, *cockeyed* means cross-eyed. Figuratively, though, the idea of slanted or twisted has expanded, so that to be foolish or absurd ("twisted" out of reason) is to be *cockeyed*.

cockney

The Modern English word *cockney* comes from Middle English *cokeney*, a combination of *coken* ("of cocks") and *ey* ("egg"), hence literally "cocks' egg." Since cocks, of course, do not lay eggs, the reason for the coining of the word is not entirely clear. But there are two reasonable possibilities: *cockney* may have been simply a child's common misnaming of a regular egg; or *cockney* may have been applied (as indeed it still is by some people) to a small or malformed egg (formerly imagined to be laid by the cock). In either case, the next step was to apply *cockney* humorously or derisively to a spoiled child or a squeamish person. Then the word was used as a derisive name for any townsman, who was regarded as squeamish and effeminate, as opposed to the sturdy country folk. Eventually *cockney* (with or without a capital *c*) was applied (and is still applied) specifically to a native of London, especially of the East End district, and to the dialect spoken there.

cock of the walk

A walk, in one sense, is an enclosed space where domestic animals can feed and exercise. In the case of a chicken walk (that is, a chicken yard), the ruler is usually a cock (rooster). Among humans, one who dominates a group or a situation, especially overbearingly, is referred to as the *cock of the walk.*

cockpit

A pit or an enclosure in which gamecocks fight is called a cockpit. Hence, any place where many arguments or battles occur is a *cockpit.* During World War I, fighter pilots began to call the pilot's compartment of an airplane a *cockpit* because of the battles fought in the air. Thus, any space on a plane or a boat used by the steersman has come to be known as a *cockpit.*

cockscomb and coxcomb

A cockscomb (or simply comb) is the crest on the head of a cock. Two objects were figuratively named by the word *cockscomb* (or, more often in these meanings, *coxcomb*) in earlier times: a professional fool's cap (which resembled the comb of a rooster in shape and color) and a person's head. Today a conceited, foolish person is sometimes called a *coxcomb.*

cocksure

Originally *cocksure* was used in an objective way and meant absolutely secure, safe, certain, or reliable. The reference was possibly to the reliability of a good faucet *(cock)* in preventing the escape of liquid. Today *cocksure* still means completely sure, but it is used subjectively—that is, according to the feeling in one's own mind.

However, people have also confused *cocksure* with *cocky,* which refers to the rooster's confident rule over the hens in the barnyard. Hence, to be arrogantly overconfident is to be *cocksure* or *cocky.*

cocky

(See *cocksure* above.)

weathercock

In German and Hungarian folklore, the cock is a weather prophet; hence, the cock's effigy was long ago often placed on secular buildings. And as a result of a ninth-century papal order, the cock's image was also placed on the spire of each church as a symbol of St. Peter's denial of Jesus before the cock crowed and as a reminder not to do likewise.

Eventually pivots were put on the cock's effigy so that it would point to the wind direction. Thus, the device is called a *weathercock*. Since the vane turns according to outside pressure, any person or thing that changes easily or often, especially to satisfy outside influences, is now figuratively a *weathercock*.

Cockle

The English word *cockle* for any of various bivalve mollusks goes back to Old French *coquille* ("shell, cockle"), an alteration (influenced by *coque*, "cock") of Latin *conchylium* ("shell"), which comes from Greek *konchylion* ("shellfish"), itself derived from *konche* ("mussel, shell"), which is based on an Indo-European root meaning "mussel, shellfish."

cockles of one's heart

Since cockles are heart-shaped bivalve mollusks, the *cockles of one's heart* are literally the valves of one's heart and figuratively one's innermost feelings. This use of *cockles* may come by way of folk etymology from New Latin *cochlea* ("ventricle"), which comes from Latin *cochlea* ("snail, snailshell," hence "winding cavity"). The expression is usually found in the phrase *to warm* (that is, to please) *the cockles of one's heart*.

Cocoon

The English word *cocoon* for the envelope about an insect larva comes from French *cocon* ("cocoon"), which goes back through Provençal *cocoun* ("cocoon," but earlier "eggshell") to Provençal *coco* ("shell") to Latin *coccum* ("kermes berry") to Greek *kokkos* ("kermes berry, kernel, pit").

cocoon

The cocoon is the covering that an insect forms about itself while passing from the larva stage to the pupa stage. Anything that suggests a cocoon, such as a physical covering or a psychological retreat, is a *cocoon*.

Colt

The Modern English word *colt* for a young male horse goes back to Old English *colt* ("young ass, young camel"), which is perhaps based on an Indo-European root meaning "to swell out" and its extensions meaning "swelling, fetus, offspring."

colt

Transferred to humans, *colt* means a young novice.

coltish

To be frisky or undisciplined, like a young horse, is to be *coltish*.

Comb

The Modern English word *comb* for a toothed instrument goes back to Old English *comb, camb* ("comb"), which are based on an Indo-European root meaning "tooth." A comb, then, is "a toothed object."

comb

The crest on the head of a domestic fowl, because of its serrate form, is called a comb. Therefore, *comb* is applied to various things resembling the cock's crest, such as the ridge of a roof or the crest of a wave.

Coot

The Modern English word *coot* for a type of bird goes back to Middle English *cote* ("coot"), which probably comes from Middle Dutch *coet* ("coot"), which may be imitative of the bird's sound.

bald as a coot

The most familiar type of coot has an extended bill that forms a broad plate on its forehead, giving it a bald appearance. A bald person, then, is said to be *(as) bald as a coot.*

coot

The coot is a water bird that looks somewhat like, and is as clumsy as, a duck. The bird has long been associated with stupidity. A foolish or irritable person (especially an old man) is sometimes called a *coot,* as in "crazy *coot,*" "old *coot,*" "silly *coot,*" and "stupid *coot.*"

Copperhead

The word *cooperhead* for a type of snake refers to the reddish brown (copper) color on the snake's head.

copperhead

In the United States, by 1775 the word *copperhead* was being applied to a kind of poisonous snake. The copperhead, even more than the related rattlesnake, developed into a symbol of something to be feared and hated. That reputation probably stems from the fact that the rattlesnake at least warns of its presence by producing a sound with the rattler on its tail. The copperhead, however, has no rattler. When disturbed, the copperhead also vibrates its tail; but the snake must have leaves under it to produce a buzzing sound. If the copperhead is on rocks, as it often is, there will be no sound, no warning. Therefore, the copperhead symbolizes the idea of vicious sneakiness, of an unexpected enemy.

That symbolism shows up in the way that the senses of the word *copperhead* have been extended through the years. By the early 1800s, any hostile, vindictive person was termed a *copperhead.* The word was also a derogatory term for any Indian (Indians being popularly associated with sneak attacks) and for any white man who lived or fought on the side of the Indians (the white man therefore being an unexpected, traitorous enemy).

In the early 1840s, *copperhead* acquired a political sense. In

Pennsylvania, one Democratic faction called another faction *Copperheads*. This use, however, soon faded. But the political use of *copperhead* was revived during the Civil War. Northern Democrats who opposed Lincoln's war policy were called *Copperheads* because in the heat of battle they were believed to be traitors (that is, unexpected enemies). The precise source for the Civil War use of the word is difficult to determine, there being so many sources to choose from. The term probably caught on with the masses simply because it brought to mind the vicious snake itself or the word's widespread figurative sense of a hostile, vindictive person. But the original Civil War coiners of the expression may have had in mind one of the word's earlier specific applications: a white man traitorously living with Indians or a Pennsylvania Democrat of the 1840s.

Or there may be yet another source. In early 1861, Alabama, after seceding from the Union, created its own national flag, on which there was a picture of a rattlesnake and the Latin motto *Noli Me Tangere* ("Dare Not Touch Me"), which sprang from a long line of similar American colonial (especially Southern) flags. Northerners, then, logically associated the Alabama rattlesnake with the whole South; and they associated the copperhead, the rattlesnake's more vicious cousin—in the popular mind, at least—with Southern sympathizers in the North. That view is supported by a quotation from an 1867 issue of the *Weekly New Mexican:* "The copperhead principle . . . hissed encouragement, in the North during the rebellion, to the less degraded rattlesnake of secession."

Today any treacherous person, especially one disloyal to a cause or a group, is a *cooperhead*.

Cow

The Modern English word *cow* for the female of various animals goes back to Old English *cu* ("cow"), which is based on an Indo-European root meaning "ox, bull, cow," probably of imitative origin.

cow

Because of the cow's flabby appearance, a coarse, untidy, overweight woman is sometimes called a *cow*.

cowcatcher

A frame fastened to the front of a railroad locomotive to shield the wheels from obstructions, such as cows, is a cowcatcher. Today a *cowcatcher* is also a brief radio/TV commercial given just before a program and advertising a secondary product of the program's sponsor; presumably the "cows" caught are the members of the audience.

cowlick

A lock or tuft of hair growing in a different direction from the rest of the hair is called a *cowlick*. Most authorities, including the major dictionaries, agree that the reason for this expression is simply that the tuft looks as though a cow had licked it.

Another view, however, is that *cowlick* comes from the way that a cow eats. A cow has a pad of cartilage, not cutting teeth, in its upper front jaw. To eat grass, a cow must wrap its tongue around a hank, twist its head, and yank off the grass. With that method of eating, a cow cannot crop as close to the ground as a sheep or some other animals can. The pattern left by a cow's "bite" has been called a cowlick, which is said by some to be the source of the figurative *cowlick*. But that source for the figurative *cowlick* is doubtful.

The *Oxford English Dictionary* records that *cowlick* goes back to at least 1598 and defines the word as meaning "a lock or curl of hair which looks as if it had been licked by a cow." In the United States, Webster, in his 1828 dictionary, defines *cowlick* as "a tuft of hair that appears as if licked by a cow." In British English slang, costermongers (people who sold food from barrows, 1500s to 1800s) used the word *cowlick* for a lock of hair that was greased, curled, brought forward from the ear, and plastered onto the cheek (as if licked into place by the tongue of a cow). That sense of the word was in use by at least the mid-1800s. In dialectal British English, *cowlick*, also in use by at least the mid-1800s, meant a lock of hair that will not lie flat on a cow's own hide, believed to be caused by "the animal constantly licking" it (*English Dialect Dictionary*, 1898).

While it is true, then, that a cow leaves rough patches of grass where it has eaten, in the minds of the users of the English language, as recorded both in British English (standard, slang, or dialectal) and American English, it is the cow's licking with its tongue that has brought about the figurative sense of *cowlick*.

holy cow

Holy cow is a mild oath that is euphemistic for *Holy Christ*. The choice of the word *cow* was probably influenced by the idea of the sacred cow in Hinduism (see *sacred cow* below).

sacred cow

In India, the cow is traditionally held to be a sacred animal. Because of that tradition, any person, object, or idea regarded as immune from criticism is called a *sacred cow*. The expression is often used sarcastically.

till the cows come home

In England, by the early 1600s it was commonly said that cows would "come home" (that is, go to the milking area) to be milked twice a day, morning and evening. The English, then, often used to say that to stay out all night (until the morning milking time) or to stay in bed all day (until the evening milking time) was to do so *till the cows come home*. That idea has broadened, so that for something to go on for a long time or forever is for it to go on *till the cows come home*.

Coyote

The English word *coyote* for a wolflike mammal comes from *coyotl* ("coyote"), of the Nahuatl language (spoken mostly in central Mexico).

coyote

The coyote, a small wolf, kills and eats sheep and calves that stray from ranches. To ranchers, then, the coyote is a hateful animal. Any hateful person, especially a cheat, can be called a *coyote*.

Crab

The Modern English word *crab* for a type of crustacean goes back to Old English *crabba* ("crab"), which is based on an Indo-European root meaning "to scratch." The crab, then, is "the scratcher."

crab, crabbed, crabby

The crab is noted for its oddly crooked walk, for its way of stubbornly hanging on to something it has seized, and for its habit of scratching things. An ill-tempered person, in reference to the animal's characteristics, is called a *crab*.

In the sport of falconry (hunting with trained hawks), when hawks fight with each other they are said *to crab* because they scratch and tear each other like crabs. That idea has been extended to humans, so that to criticize (one)—that is, "to tear (one) to pieces" with words—is *to crab* (one). And to complain is *to crab*. To head an airplane into a crosswind in an apparently sideways motion (like a crab's walk) is *to crab* the plane.

The senses deriving from *crab* for a crustacean have been mixed with those from *crab* for a kind of sour apple. That mixture is especially evident in the adjectives *crabbed*, meaning contrary or ill-tempered or bitter or hard to make out, and *crabby*, meaning sour-natured or complaining.

Crane

The Modern English word *crane* for a long-necked bird goes back to Old English *cran* ("crane"), which is based on an Indo-European root meaning "crane" and "to cry hoarsely." The crane, then, is named for its harsh voice.

crane

Because of the crane's long neck, a long-necked machine for lifting heavy weights is also called a *crane*. And to stretch one's neck, as if to see something, is *to crane* it.

Craw

The Modern English word *craw* for the crop (a pouch in the throat) of a bird comes from Middle English *crawe* ("craw"), which goes back to Old English unrecorded *craga* ("throat"), which is based on an Indo-European root meaning "to swallow."

stick in the craw

The craw, a pouchlike enlargement in the throat of a bird, is a place where food is held and prepared for digestion. Transferring that idea to humans, people sometimes say that for something to be hard to accept (that is, "hard to swallow") is for it *to stick in the* (or *one's) craw.*

Crest

The English word *crest* for the tuft on top of the head of an animal (such as the comb of a rooster) goes back to Latin *crista* ("crest"), which is based on an Indo-European root meaning "to bend, turn, twist." A crest, then, is named for its flexibility.

crest

As the crest represents the top of the rooster's (or other animal's) head, so the word *crest* can represent the highest part of anything, such as the top of a mountain, the high point of a wave, an ornament on top of a helmet, or even the final or most intense point of an action or a process (such as the *crest* of an athlete's ability).

crestfallen

A rooster with a drooping crest is said to be crestfallen. That image is often applied to humans, so that to be sad or discouraged is to be *crestfallen.*

Crocodile

The English word *crocodile* for a type of reptile goes back to Greek *krokodilos* ("lizard," especially "lizard of the Nile," that is, "crocodile"). The Greek word is a combination of two other Greek words: *kroke* ("pebble") and *drilos* ("worm"). The crocodile, then, is literally "the pebble worm," so named by the Greeks because the supposedly wormlike lizards and crocodiles commonly sun themselves on smooth stones.

after while, crocodile

(See *alligator* under "Alligator.")

crocodile tears

In folklore, it is said that crocodiles shed tears over those they devour. In one version of that belief, crocodiles cry or moan to lure potential victims. Another version says that the crocodiles shed tears of sorrow while eating their prey. In a third version, the sorrowful tears come after the eating. In any case, the crocodiles do not take their own tears seriously enough to refrain from devouring their victims. Today, then, insincere sorrow or tears are called *crocodile tears*.

Crow

The Modern English word *crow* for a kind of bird goes back to Old English *crawe* ("crow"), which is based on an Indo-European root meaning "to cry hoarsely." The crow, then, is named for its harsh voice.

as the crow flies

In folklore, the crow is noted for its straight flight. Therefore, to go in a straight line or by the most direct route is to go *as the crow flies*.

crowbar

The *crowbar* is an iron or steel bar, usually pointed at one end and flattened and slightly bent at the other. The name refers to the ends of the tool: the pointed end looks like the bird's beak; and the other end, when shaped into a two-pronged fork, looks like the bird's foot.

crow's-feet

Wrinkles around the corners of human eyes, because the

shapes of the lines may look like a crow's footprints, are called *crow's-feet*.

crow's nest

A lookout station near the top of a mast on a ship is called a *crow's nest*. Any similar station ashore, such as that for a traffic officer, is also known as a *crow's nest*.

eat crow

In an anecdote set during the War of 1812, it is said that a British officer and a Yankee took turns forcing the other to eat a raw crow. Either from that story or, more likely, from a simple reference to the bad taste of crow meat comes the idea of saying that to be forced to do something unpleasant or embarrassing, such as to retract a statement (that is, to "eat" one's words), is *to eat crow*.

Cub

The origin of the word *cub* for the young of the bear and various other animals is uncertain. But *cub* may come from a Scandinavian source. In Old Norse and Modern Icelandic, for example, *kobbi* means "young seal" (denoting a heavy and clumsy form); Norwegian *kubbe* is "block, stump, chunk of log"; and Swedish dialectal *kubb* is "log of wood." If these Scandinavian words are related to *cub*, then the idea behind the English word *cub* would be shapelessness, the baby animal being thought of as a little block of wobbly fur (for a similar idea about bear cubs, see *lick into shape* under "Animal-related Expressions" in Part Two). The Scandinavian words are based on an Indo-European root meaning "a hollow place, a round object, a lump."

cub

A young and inexperienced person can be called a *cub*, as in "*cub* scout" and "*cub* reporter."

Cuckoo

The word *cuckoo* for a type of bird comes from an attempt to imitate the sound of the bird's call.

cuckold

Among some types of cuckoos, the female, rather than making a home with her mate, lays her eggs in the nests of birds of other species. Polyandry (as well as polygamy) is also common among some cuckoos. The female cuckoo, then, has come to symbolize an unfaithful wife, and a betrayed husband is known as a *cuckold* (*-old* is adapted from an Old French pejorative suffix).

cuckoo

Cuckoos are primarily noted for two characteristics: their monotonous "coo-coo" call and the habit among some types of cuckoos of laying their eggs in the nests of birds of other species, which hatch and raise the young cuckoos. Both characteristics make the cuckoo seem strange. Adding to that image is the familiar cuckoo clock, in which the mechanical bird's cry and jerky movements suggest something clownishly crazy. Therefore, a silly or crazy person is said to be a *cuckoo*.

Cud

Cud is the food brought up into the mouth from the first stomach and chewed again by a ruminating animal (ruminants include such animals as cattle, buffalo, deer, and camels). The Modern English word *cud* goes back to Old English *cudu* ("cud"), which is based on an Indo-European root meaning "to bend, curve, arch." Cud, then, is named for its being easily bent or molded.

chew the cud

A ruminating animal has a special section in its stomach (see "Rumen") where food is stored and partially broken down. The animal can bring the food back up into its mouth and chew the cud (the food) again. Figuratively, among humans, to think about something (especially something already done or said) over and over again is *to chew the cud*.

Cur

The Modern English word *cur* for a dog comes from

Middle English *curre* ("cur"), itself from the earlier Middle English word *kurdogge*, which is a combination of *kur* (of uncertain origin, but probably related to the Old Norse imitative verb *kurra*, "to growl," which is based on an Indo-European root meaning "to cry hoarsely") plus Middle English *dogge* ("dog"). A cur, then, is "a growler."

cur

The word *cur* was formerly applied without contempt to any dog, especially a watchdog or a shepherd's dog. But the word has come to refer to a dog that is worthless or unfriendly. A despicable or cowardly person is sometimes called a *cur*.

Dinosaur

The English word *dinosaur* for any of a group of extinct reptiles comes from a combination of Greek *deinos* ("terrible, frightful") and *sauros* ("lizard"). The dinosaur, then, is "the terrible lizard."

dinosaur

Dinosaurs are popularly noted for two characteristics: their large size and their sudden extinction. Today anything that is extinct or nearly extinct, especially if it was once powerful or popular, is often called a *dinosaur*.

Dodo

The English word *dodo* for a type of extinct bird comes from Portuguese *doudo* ("dodo bird"), which comes from the Portuguese adjective *doudo* ("silly, stupid"). The bird is so named because of its clumsy behavior and odd appearance.

dead as a dodo

The dodo, as an extinct bird, is a "dead" species. That fact and the catchy alliteration of the *d*'s in *dead* and *dodo* account for the common expression *(as) dead as a dodo*, meaning certainly dead. (See *dead as a herring* under "Herring" for more about phrases beginning *dead as*.)

dodo

The dodo was found on the island of Mauritius in the Indian Ocean. The bird had a clumsy turkey-sized body and stubby wings that could not get the creature off the ground. In a fairly short time, the dodo was killed off by men and by the hogs, rats, and dogs that the men carried with them to the island home of the dodo. Since the dodo was helpless and apparently dull witted, it became common to refer to a slow-thinking person as a *dodo*.

Dog

The Modern English word *dog* for the common domesticated mammal comes from Old English *docga* ("dog"), perhaps originally an imitation of the dog's bark.

barking dogs seldom bite

Some dogs bark fiercely though they are afraid actually to attack. The expression *barking dogs seldom* (or *never*) *bite* refers to people who sound more dangerous than they really are.

better to be a live dog than a dead lion

The dog is sometimes thought of as a cowardly animal (see *dog* below), whereas the lion is the courageous "king of the jungle." To say that it is better to be careful (even cowardly) than to take unnecessary (though courageous) risks is to say that it is *better to be a live dog than a dead lion*.

call off the dogs

When dogs are pursuing or attacking the wrong object, they must be called off by the owner. Therefore, to stop any unpleasant procedure is *to call off the dogs*.

cat-and-dog

(See *cat-and-dog* under "Cat.")

dog

Though the dog is often called "man's best friend," the animal has a long history of being referred to in unpleasant terms. In the Bible, for example, troops of dogs are pictured wandering the streets eating dead bodies and other offal. Thus, hated enemies are called *dogs*, as in Psalms 22:16: "For dogs have compassed me: the assembly of the wicked have inclosed me." Dogs became symbols of degradation, as in Matthew 7:6: "Give not that which is holy unto the dogs, neither cast ye your pearls before swine."

A worthless, cowardly, or degraded man has long been called a *dog*. A cruel term for an ugly, boring, or crude woman is also *dog*. On the other hand, the word is sometimes applied playfully, as in "sly *dog*" and "lucky *dog*."

To follow or chase, as a hunting dog tracks its quarry, is *to dog*.

As an adjective, *dog* can mean inferior, as in "*dog* rhyme," "*dog* English," and "*dog* Latin."

dog days

Dog days is a translation of Latin *dies caniculares*, itself a translation of Greek *hemerai kynades*. The term refers to a period in July and August when the ancients reckoned the sun to rise at the same time as the Dog Star (Sirius). That period was believed to be the hottest and most unwholesome time of the year because the Dog Star (the brightest, and therefore in folk belief the "hottest," in the sky) added its heat to that of the sun. The *dog days* have also long been associated with the popular belief that dogs are most likely to go mad during that period of time.

Today any hot, sultry day can be called a *dog day*. Figuratively, *dog days* are any period of dullness or lack of progress.

dog-ear

Because it looks like the ear of a dog, the turned-down corner of a page is called a *dog-ear*.

dog-eat-dog

When human competition is as fierce as a dogfight, people are acting in a *dog-eat-dog* way.

dogface

Dogface is American slang for a soldier, especially an infantryman. In England, *dog-faced*, meaning having a face like a dog's, and *dog's face*, a general term of abuse, had been in common use long before the American expression developed.

dogfight

Any physical battle can be called a *dogfight*.

dogged

From the dog has come the idea that to be stubborn is to be *dogged*.

doggerel

Trivial poetry, especially of a burlesque nature, is called *doggerel*. *Dog* may here be used in an animal-related contemptuous sense, meaning bad. But there is also evidence that it may come from Latin or Italian *doga* ("barrel stave") and be merely influenced by *dog* meaning the animal; *doggerel* would then be parallel with similar words in some other languages, such as German *Knüttelvers* ("cudgel verse").

doggone

Doggone is a euphemism for *God damn*. The form of *doggone* may have evolved from the earlier phrase *dog on it* (a form of imprecation) or from Scottish *dagone* ("gone to the dogs").

dog in the manger

In one of Aesop's fables, a dog fell asleep on the hay in the manger of an ox. Later the hungry ox entered the stall and tried to eat. But the dog, angry because it had been awakened, barked and snapped and would not let the ox eat the hay. Finally the ox said, "Dog, if you wanted to eat my dinner, I would have no objection. But you will neither eat it yourself nor let me enjoy it." Today anyone who neither enjoys a thing nor allows others to enjoy it is called a *dog in the manger*.

dog it

Dogs are sometimes pictured as being lazy or useless. Hence, to fail to do one's best is *to dog it*.

dogleg

Something having a sharp angle or bend like that in a dog's hind leg is a *dogleg*. A sharp bend in a road, for example, is a *dogleg*, as is a golf hole having an angled fairway.

dogmeat

Meat fit only for a dog is *dogmeat*. Extended, *dogmeat* refers to anything disliked.

dog paddle

One simple swimming stroke is executed by paddling both arms underwater while kicking the legs. Since that method looks like the typical way a dog swims, the stroke is called the *dog paddle*.

dogs

Dogs is slang for feet.

dog's life

A dog is often pictured as being abused and enslaved by its master. Anyone, then, who lives an unhappy, dull existence is said to live a *dog's life*.

dog tag

A dog tag is an identification tag for a dog. Extended to humans, *dog tag* means a military identification tag worn about the neck by a soldier.

dog-tired

To be as tired as a dog is after a long chase is to be *dog-tired*.

dogtown

A colony of prairie dogs is called a dogtown. In American theater slang, *dogtown* refers to a small city used for tryouts before a metropolitan presentation.

every dog has his day

A proverbial way of saying that even the lowliest person may have a time of action or a period of power and influence is *every dog has his* (or *its*) *day.*

This is said to be originally a Macedonian proverb going back to 406 B.C. and the death of the Greek dramatist Euripides, who was killed by a pack of dogs set upon him by a rival.

go to the dogs

To go to the dogs means to go to ruin, morally or physically. This is an old expression, the form in ancient Greece being *to go to the crows.* The modern use of *to go to the dogs* has many interrelated sources. For one, the Bible often depicts dogs as degraded creatures (see *dog* above); therefore, to become degraded (that is, to go to moral ruin) is *to go to the dogs.* Another source is the fact that dogs are often tossed old, decaying scraps of food; therefore, to decay (that is, to go to physical ruin) is to fall apart to such an extent as to be worth nothing but to be tossed to the dogs, that is, *to go to the dogs.* Perhaps the main idea, though, is simply that the dog represents a low condition in life; therefore, to go to a low point (that is, to go to moral or physical ruin) is *to go to the dogs.*

a hair of the dog that bit you

There was once a popular belief that the only cure for a mad dog's bite was its own hair. Today, then, a cure based on the source of the problem, especially another drink of liquor to overcome drunkenness, is *a hair of the dog that bit you.*

hangdog

Formerly, *hangdog* referred to a person fit only to hang a dog or to be hung like a dog. Now any contemptible, sneaky person is a *hangdog.*

As an adjective, *hangdog* means contemptible, ashamed, dejected.

hot dog

In the late 1800s, *frankfurter* (after Frankfurt, Germany)

was applied to a kind of sausage sandwich. By 1896 the sandwich was called a *red hot* because it was served hot, the name being popularized especially at New York City's Polo Grounds. In the early 1900s, Hearst cartoonist T.A. Dorgan popularized the name *hot dog* when he drew a cartoon of the sausage in the form of a dachshund on a bun (a dachshund being at the time a symbol for anything German), fancifully hinting that the meat was made from dog flesh.

However, the phrase *hot dog* was already in existence before it was applied to the sausage. The 1870s brought the phrase *to put on the dog* (see *put on the dog* below), meaning to show off, in which *dog* stood for high style or pretentiousness. Soon *dog* was being used alone, as in this quotation from 1889: "He's made the thing awfully *chic;* it's jimminy; there's lots of dog about it." At the same time, *hot* was beginning to mean good or skillful. By the mid-1890s, *hot* and *dog* were combined, as in this from 1896: "*Hot-dog,* good, superior. 'He has made some hot-dog drawings for——.'" *Hot dog* was also a noun meaning one skilled in something, especially with the connotation of being a show-off.

Hot dog as an exclamation of approval or surprise was in use by the early 1900s. Soon thereafter came its intensification: *hot diggity dog.* This interjection may have evolved from either the noun *hot dog* meaning sausage or the adjective *hot-dog* meaning good, superior.

In surfing slang since the 1950s, *hot dog* means a kind of board, so named from its weinerlike shape. Spinning off from the earlier *hot dog* meaning a skillful show-off, *to hot-dog* means to do stunts on the board; the rider is a *hot dogger* and the action is *hot dogging.* (Other origins suggested for these surfing senses are the interjection *hot dog* and 1890s college slang *dogs* meaning feet and its extension *to hot dog* meaning to go fast.)

in the doghouse

To be *in the doghouse* is to be in disgrace or in a state of being punished. The origin of this expression may be simply the obvious image of a scolded dog retreating to its doghouse. But the popularity of the phrase seems to have been generated by an incident in James M. Barrie's famous play *Peter Pan* (1904). In *Peter Pan*, Mr. Darling's children have a nurse named Nana, who (in this fantasy) happens to be a Newfoundland dog. The children want Nana to continue living in the main house; but Mr. Darling, jealous of Nana's influence in his home, wants her to live in the doghouse. Finally he drags her out and chains her up. Then the children run (or, more precisely, fly) away from home with Peter Pan. Mr. Darling, feeling responsible for his children's flight, decides to punish himself by crawling into the doghouse with the intention of staying there until the children return.

let sleeping dogs lie

Sleeping dogs can be thought of as potential enemies that one should not wake up. So, too, to avoid disturbing a presently quiet but possibly dangerous person or situation is *to let sleeping dogs lie.*

put on the dog

The origin of this expression is uncertain, but the phrase may come from the fact that some aristocrats used to carry little dogs (especially spaniels) about with them. Therefore, among "ordinary" people, to be ostentatious is *to put on the dog.* (See also *hot dog* above.)

rain cats and dogs

(See *rain cats and dogs* under "Cat.")

red dog

In football, linebackers usually stay in the defensive backfield during plays. But sometimes they cross the line of scrimmage to rush the passer. Since they chase (or "hunt," like hunting dogs) the passer, the linebackers are said *to dog.* In the early days of football, there was a famous dogging system using a color code: red meant one linebacker was supposed to rush; blue, two; and green, three. Therefore, to send in one linebacker was *to red dog.* Later *red dog* referred to dogging by any number of linebackers. Today the word *red* is often dropped.

see a man about a dog

A jocular way of making an excuse for leaving a person or a place is to say that one has *to see a man about a dog*. The expression dates from at least 1866, when Dion Boucicault used it in the play *Flying Scud*.

shaggy-dog story

A long story with an unexpected ending, impressive to the teller but boring to the listener, is a *shaggy-dog story*, so named from the shaggy dog featured in many such stories of the 1940s.

sick as a dog

One characteristic of many dogs is that they tend to lick up their own vomit. The Bible refers to that trait in Proverbs 26:11 and 2 Peter 2:22. Since the vomiting obviously implies that the dogs are ill, dogs are often associated with sickness itself. Therefore, to be ill is to be *(as) sick as a dog*.

stay until the last dog is hung

To remain until the very last is *to stay until the last dog is hung*. The origin of this expression is apparently unknown. But the phrase may be a jocular expansion of the earlier *hangdog* (see *hangdog* above) since a person staying a long time may well end up with a tired, "hangdog" countenance. Or the phrase may be a reference to American Old West lynching parties, at which an avid spectator would be certain to stay until the last dog (criminal) was hung.

straight as a dog's hind leg

To be crooked or unreliable is to be *(as) straight as a dog's hind leg* (which, of course, is actually bent).

tail wagging the dog

When an unimportant member of a group controls everyone else, he is said to be a *tail wagging the dog*.

top dog

In a dogfight, especially in dogfighting as a "sport," the

winning dog is the one that ends on top of the losing dog. Therefore, someone believed to have the highest power (based on previous records) is called a *top dog,* while someone thought likely to be beaten (based on previous records) is called an *underdog.*

underdog

(See *top dog* above.)

watchdog

A watchdog is a dog that guards people and/or property. Hence, a person or a group that guards against any undesirable practices is a *watchdog.*

water dog

A water dog is a dog accustomed to the water, especially when trained to retrieve waterfowl. Hence, a person (such as a sailor) who is at ease in or on water is a *water dog.*

you can't teach an old dog new tricks

You can't teach an old dog new tricks is said about a person who cannot or will not learn new ways of doing things.

Dolphin

The English word *dolphin* for a kind of small whale goes back through French and Latin forms to Greek *delphis* (stem *delphin-,* "dolphin"), which comes from *delphys* ("womb"), which is based on an Indo-European root meaning "womb." The dolphin is so named because of its womblike shape.

dolphin

A buoy for mooring boats is called a *dolphin,* as is a cluster of piles used as a dock fender or a mooring or a guide for boats.

dolphin kick

The swimming movement of kicking both legs up and down simultaneously is called the *dolphin kick.* Two *dolphin kicks* are performed during each *butterfly stroke.* (See also *butterfly stroke* under "Butterfly.")

Donkey

The origin of the word *donkey* for the ass is uncertain, but there are two main theories. One is that *donkey* comes from a combination of English *dun* ("brownish gray," the animal's typical color) and *-key* ("little," as in *monkey*). The second theory is that *donkey* is a pet variation of the human name *Duncan* (*dun* again being associated with the animal's color).

donkey

Donkey is a common word today for the ass (see "Ass"). A stupid, silly, or stubborn person is sometimes called a *donkey*.

donkey engine

The donkey is smaller than its relatives the horse and the mule. From that fact comes the idea of calling a small auxiliary engine or a small locomotive used in switching a *donkey engine*.

donkeywork

Monotonous, routine work (like a donkey's) is called *donkeywork*.

Dove

The Modern English word *dove* for a type of bird comes from Middle English *dove, dofe, duve* ("dove"), which may go back to Old English *dufe* as recorded only in *dufedoppa* ("a diving waterfowl," literally "dip-diver," from *dufan*, "to dive," and *doppa*, "dipper"). Other authorities, however, say that *dufe* goes back to an Indo-European root meaning "smoky, dark," the dove being originally "the dark-colored bird."

dove

The dove, a type of pigeon, has long been noted for its gentleness and harmlessness. A person who is tender, innocent, or loving (especially a woman or a child) is often called a *dove*.

The dove is an ancient symbol of peace, as in the biblical story of Noah's Ark (Genesis 8:8-12), in which the dove returned with the olive branch of peace between God and man. Therefore, one who prefers talking rather than fighting (especially in international conflicts) is called a *dove*. (Contrast *hawk* under "Hawk.")

dovetail

Anything that looks like a dove's tail (that is, something V-shaped and interlocking) can be called a *dovetail*, such as a V-like or wedgelike piece of wood that fits snugly into another piece. To join two or more things or ideas together to form a whole is *to dovetail* them.

flutter the dovecotes

A dovecote is a structure, usually above the ground, where doves, or pigeons, are kept. A settled, conservative, quiet group or institution is sometimes called a *dovecote*. And to cause a stir in such a group or an institution is *to flutter the dovecotes*.

Down

The English word *down* for the soft plumage of birds goes back to Old Norse *dunn* ("down"), which is based on an Indo-European root meaning "to fly about like dust, whirl." Down, then, is named for its tendency to float in the air.

down

Down is the soft feathers forming the first plumage of a young bird and underlying the contour feathers in an adult bird. Any similar material—such as the first signs of a beard on a young man or the pubescence on plants and fruits—can be called *down*.

downy

Downy is an adjective describing anything made of or resembling the down of birds. Figuratively, anything soft or soothing can be described as being *downy*.

Drone

The Modern English word *drone* for a male bee goes back

to Old English *dran* ("drone"), which is based on an Indo-European root meaning "to drone, murmur, buzz."

drone

A drone is a male bee that has no sting, performs no work, and produces no honey. An idler or one who lives off others is therefore called a *drone.* A *drone* is also a pilotless aircraft operated by remote control.

The sound of the drone is evidently the source of the verb *to drone,* meaning to make a continuous deep humming or buzzing sound. Extended, *to drone* means to speak in a monotonous tone. *To drone* yields the noun *drone,* meaning a continuous low sound, a pipe on a bagpipe tuned to produce a single tone, or (in music) any sustained tone.

Duck

The Modern English noun *duck* for a type of bird goes back to Old English *duce* ("duck"), which is related to the Middle English verb *duken* ("to dive"). The duck, then, is "the diver," so named for its "ducking" movements in the water.

as a duck takes to water

A duck is naturally comfortable in water. Therefore, when a person has a natural talent for something, it can be said that he takes to it *as a duck takes to water.*

dead duck

The expression *dead duck* probably evolved (helped by the alliteration of the *d*'s) from the earlier expression *like a (dying) duck in a thunderstorm,* which means having a forlorn and helpless appearance and is a reference to ducklings that die in rainstorms because they are not yet fully protected by body oils. *Dead duck* can refer to a dead person, but more often today it refers simply to a person who is trapped in a bad situation (compare *sitting duck* below).

duck

Duck is sometimes used as an informal word for a person, as in "He's an odd (or strange) *duck.*"

ducks and drakes

There is a pastime of throwing flat stones across water so as to make them skip over the surface several times before sinking. Since the movements of the stones resemble the actions of waterfowl, the game is called *ducks and drakes*. And since the essence of the pastime is to throw things (the stones) away and let them sink, it is also said that to waste something (especially money) is to play *ducks and drakes* with it.

duck soup

Something easy to do or someone easy to conquer is *duck soup*. The origin of this expression is uncertain. It may refer to the idea that ducks are so naturally fatty that they are easily made up into soup. Or it may be related to *sitting duck* (see *sitting duck* below); a sitting duck is easy to shoot and will therefore easily make a pot of duck soup.

ducktail

There is a style of haircut in which the hair is worn long on the sides and combed to meet at the back. This haircut, because it resembles the tail of a duck, is called a *ducktail*.

ducky

Ducky, a cute or childlike form of the animal word *duck*, is a term of endearment, like *dear* or *darling*. It can also mean fine (often used ironically), as in "Everything is just *ducky*."

fine day for ducks

Since ducks enjoy water, a rainy day is said to be a *fine day for ducks*.

lame duck

A disabled, helpless, or ineffective person or thing has long been compared to a wounded fowl and called a *lame duck*. There have been two important kinds of specific *lame ducks*. In eighteenth-century London, stockbrokers who lost their money were called *lame ducks* because they were said to "waddle" out of the building like wounded ducks. In the United States, an elected official who completes his term in office after an election in which he has failed to be reelected is also called a *lame duck;* that is, he "waddles" through the rest of his term like a wounded duck.

sitting duck

A sitting duck is one resting on water; it is easy to shoot. Therefore, any helpless or open target or victim is a *sitting duck.*

ugly duckling

A person or a thing that appears unpromising but that develops, or has the potential to develop, worthy qualities is an *ugly duckling.* The source of the expression is Hans Christian Andersen's story "The Ugly Duckling."

water off a duck's back

A duck, like other birds, spreads an oil on its feathers. The oil causes water to roll off, rather than soak into, a duck's plumage. Anything, then, that has little or no effect is said to be *water off a duck's back.*

Eagle

The English word *eagle* for a type of bird goes back to Latin *aquila* ("eagle").

eagle

In golf, a score of two below par on a hole is an *eagle.* (Compare *birdie* under "Bird.")

eagle eye, eagle-eyed

The eagle has extremely keen eyesight. A person who has sharp vision or who watches something closely is said to be an *eagle eye.* The person's sharp eyesight itself is also an *eagle eye,* as in "He watched her with an *eagle eye.*"

Eagle-eyed is the adjective form.

eaglestone

A nodule of ironstone about the size of a walnut is an *eaglestone,* so named from the belief that an eagle keeps such a stone in its nest to facilitate hatching.

spread eagle, spread-eagle

A common sign for various states and rulers has long been the spread eagle, that is, a picture of an eagle with wings raised and legs extended. Something resembling or suggestive of that image is also a *spread eagle,* especially a skating figure executed with the skates placed heel to heel in a straight line.

Among humans, to stand or move with the arms and legs stretched out is *to spread-eagle.* A skater, for example, *spread-eagles* to perform certain acrobatic figures. The verb also has a transitive sense: to stretch out or spread over is *to spread-eagle;* prisoners have been *spread-eagled* and tied down to be flogged.

In reference to the spread eagle on the Great Seal of the United States, the adjective *spread-eagle* means marked by boastful exaggeration, especially of the greatness of the United States.

Egg

The English word *egg* for a reproductive body comes from Old Norse *egg* ("egg"), which is based on an Indo-European root meaning "of a bird," which in turn comes from a root meaning "bird."

all one's eggs in one basket

To gamble everything on one scheme is to put *all (of) one's eggs in one basket.* This expression probably comes from the fable about the woman who carried all of her hopes for the future in one basket full of eggs, which she dropped while on the way to market (see *count one's chickens before they are hatched* under "Chicken").

egg

A person is sometimes referred to as an *egg*, as in "He's a good (or bad) *egg*."

egghead

An intellectual is sometimes called an *egghead*. The reference is to the popular idea that a person with a high forehead (producing an egg-shaped appearance) is supposed to be highly intelligent. The expression seems to have originated during the 1952 presidential campaign of Adlai Stevenson, who was supported by many intellectuals *(eggheads)* and was himself largely bald and quite intellectual (especially when compared with most aspirants to the presidency).

goose egg

(See *lay an egg* below.)

kill the goose that laid the golden eggs

There are many different versions of a fable about a goose that laid golden eggs. In one version, the farmer who owned the goose killed it to get all of the golden eggs at once. But there were no eggs inside; and the dead goose, of course, could lay no more. Therefore, it is now said that to destroy a good, steady supply of something valuable while trying to make a greedy, temporary gain is *to kill the goose that laid* (or *lays*) *the golden eggs*.

lay an egg

In the British game of cricket, a score of zero has, since at least the mid-1800s, been called a *duck's egg* because of the egg's resemblance to a zero. By the 1860s, that idea had been adapted by Americans for the game of baseball, in which the term was changed to *goose egg*. To fail to score, then, was *to lay an egg* on the scoreboard. Today to fail at anything is *to lay an egg*.

nest egg

A natural or artificial egg left in a nest to encourage a

fowl to lay more eggs is called a nest egg. Therefore, a fund of extra money (like an extra egg in the nest) is a *nest egg*.

teach one's grandmother to suck eggs

In seventeenth-century England, *to grope a goose* (or other poultry) meant to examine it to see if it had eggs. An elderly woman on a farm would presumably have plenty of experience at such groping. Therefore, it was commonly said that to presume to give advice to someone more experienced was *to teach one's grandmother to grope a goose* (*duck*, etc.). By the early eighteenth century, the expression had become the modern *to teach one's grandmother to suck eggs* or *to tell one's grandmother how to suck eggs*.

walk on eggs

To be careful about anything is *to walk on* (or *upon*) *eggs*.

with egg on one's face

To be in an embarrassing or humiliating situation is to be *with egg on one's face*. The origin of the phrase is uncertain. But two possibilities have been suggested: a reference to an actor who has had rotten eggs thrown into his face or a reference to an animal (such as a weasel) that comes out of a henhouse with egg on its face as proof of its thievery.

Elephant

The English word *elephant* for a type of huge mammal goes back to Greek *elephas* ("ivory," later "elephant"), which is a compound of *el-* (related to Hamitic *elu*, "elephant") and *-ephas* (related to Egyptian *abu*, "elephant, ivory"). The elephant, then, is originally "the ivory beast," referring to the animal's ivory tusks.

elephantiasis

Elephantiasis is Latin for a kind of leprosy in which the skin takes on the appearance of an elephant's hide. In English, the word has come to mean an enlargement and thickening of tissues. The sense of the word has extended, so that now any undesirable large growth (such as in an institution) is *elephantiasis*.

elephantine

Elephantine means massive or clumsy.

memory of an elephant

Elephants are intelligent and have fairly good memories. Furthermore, elephants live quite a long time, up to sixty years. Those two ideas have combined to produce a common though overstated expression: to be able to remember things for a long time is to have the *memory of an elephant*.

see the elephant

The elephant is a symbol of largeness and therefore fullness. Hence, to gain experience in life, to see the sights, or to have enough is *to see the elephant*.

white elephant

In Siam (now Thailand), the white elephant was a rare, sacred animal. Its food was served on huge gold-and-silver platters, and its water was scented with jasmine. It was covered with ceremonial garments, and it rode on a special float. Each one born became the automatic property of the king. Furthermore, it was forbidden by law for anyone to work or kill a white elephant. To ruin someone he disliked, a king would simply give the person a white elephant as a gift. The recipient could neither use the beast for work nor kill it. Eventually the elephant's tremendous appetite would drive the person into poverty. Today any costly but useless possession can be called a *white elephant*.

Ermine

The English word *ermine* for a type of weasel is adopted from Old French *ermine* (feminine of *ermin*, "ermine"). The French word may be derived from Latin *Armenius* as used in the expression *Armenius mus* ("Armenian mouse"), which goes back to Greek *Armenia*, the name of a region in western Asia. Another possible origin for the French word is Middle High German *hermin* ("erminelike"), which goes back to Old High German *harmo* ("ermine, weasel"), which corresponds to Old English *hearma* ("ermine, weasel").

ermine

In some parts of the world, high officials—such as kings, peers, judges—wear, or used to wear, robes trimmed with ermine. Thus, such an official's rank or office itself is sometimes referred to as an *ermine,* as in "The public no longer trusted the judicial *ermine.*"

Fawn

The English word *fawn* for a young deer goes back through French and Vulgar Latin forms to Latin *fetus* ("offspring"), which is based on an Indo-European root meaning "to suck."

fawn

From the color of the young deer comes the idea of referring to a light grayish brown as *fawn.*

Feather

The Modern English word *feather* for a bird covering goes back to Old English *fether* ("feather"), which is based on an Indo-European root meaning "wing, feather," which in turn is based on a root meaning "to fly."

birds of a feather flock together

(See *birds of a feather flock together* under "Bird.")

feather

Anything extremely light or insignificant is a *feather.* A tuft of hair, especially a fringe of long hair on the legs of some dogs and horses, is a *feather.* A feathery flaw in the eye or in a gem is a *feather.* A condition or mood can be called a *feather* (see *in fine feather* below).

In rowing, to turn the oar blades parallel to the water on the backstroke is *to feather* the oars. In aviation, to change the angle of the propeller blades so that the chords are parallel to the line of flight is *to feather* the blades. Both senses are references to the appearance of a bird's feather.

featherbed

A featherbed is a bed stuffed with feathers (or down). In union-industry relations, to require an employer by a union rule to hire more workers than are necessary is *to featherbed*, the expression suggesting that the extra workers might as well lie about on a featherbed.

featherbrain

A feather is so light that it seems to have little substance. A person with little substance in his brain—that is, a foolish or scatterbrained person—can be called a *featherbrain*.

feather in one's cap

Among many Asians and American Indians, it was an ancient custom for a person to add a feather to his cap (or any headdress) every time he slew an enemy. In Europe in the Middle Ages, a feather in one's cap or helmet was a mark of distinction, especially for action on the battlefield. In England, the feather custom received much attention when Edward the "Black Prince" of Wales defeated an enemy and won a crest of three ostrich feathers, which thereafter became a symbol for each Prince of Wales. Because of all of these traditions, any honor can be called a *feather in one's cap*.

feather one's nest

Many birds line their nests with soft down (tiny feathers) from their own breasts. Among humans, to make things comfortable for oneself (sometimes by dishonest means) is *to feather one's nest*.

featherweight

In professional boxing, a fighter weighing from 123 to 126 pounds is called a *featherweight*. A *featherweight* is also someone who is insignificant, unintelligent, or ineffective.

fuss and feathers

In the mid-1800s, the American general Winfield Scott was given the nickname Old Fuss and Feathers because of his ostentatiousness (fuss) and his vanity about his appearance (*feathers*). Soon the expression was applied generally, so that any form of pretentious display or vanity is *fuss and feathers.*

in fine feather

A bird usually looks its best when it has all of its feathers, that is, when it is not molting. Therefore, among humans, to be ornately dressed or to be in good condition physically, emotionally, financially, or otherwise is to be *in fine* (or *full* or *good* or *high*) *feather.*

light as a feather

Anything extremely light in weight can be said to be *(as) light as a feather.*

make the feathers fly

To cause a disturbance is, in reference to fighting birds, *to make the feathers fly.*

ruffled feathers

When birds are excited, they sometimes ruffle (puff up) their feathers, as during courtship or in moments of anger. Figuratively, an excited person can be said to have *ruffled feathers,* as in "Don't *ruffle* his *feathers,*" "Don't get your *feathers ruffled,*" and "Smooth his *ruffled feathers.*"

show the white feather

In a gamecock, a white feather under the colored feathers in the tail is said to indicate a bird of inferior breeding. In a fight, such a bird will quickly drop its tail and show its white feather to admit defeat. It is said of humans, then, that to act cowardly is *to show the white feather.*

you could have knocked me over with a feather

You could (or *might*) *have knocked me over* (or *down*) *with a feather* is a way of expressing surprise.

Feline

The English word *feline* meaning pertaining to cats goes

back to Latin *feles* ("cat"), which is of uncertain origin, though a possible source may be hinted at in Egyptian *pekhat* ("Cat-Goddess").

feline

The adjective *feline* is used to describe the characteristics of the cat family, *Felidae*, which consists of lions, tigers, leopards, domestic cats, and others. Any human conduct that is catlike, sly, or treacherous can be described as being *feline*.

Ferret

The English word *ferret* for a type of polecat goes back to Vulgar Latin *furittus* ("little thief"), a diminutive of Latin *fur* ("thief"), which is based on an Indo-European root meaning "to carry." The ferret, then, is originally "the one that carries off (steals)" things, so named because the animal likes to steal domestic eggs.

ferret out

For centuries, people have been training the ferret to drive burrowing animals (such as rabbits and rats) out of their holes. Among humans, to search out or bring to light is *to ferret out*, as in *"to ferret out the truth."*

Filly

The English word *filly* for a young female horse goes back to Old Norse *fylja* ("filly"), which is based on an Indo-European root meaning "little, few."

filly

A lively young woman or girl is called a *filly*.

Fin

The Modern English word *fin* for a fish's propeller-guide goes back to Old English *finn* ("fin"), which is based on an Indo-European root meaning "something pointed."

fin

Anything resembling the fin of a fish—such as a finlike structure on a submarine or a surface vessel, a ridge on a radiator, or even a human arm or hand—can be called a *fin*.

Fish

The Modern English word *fish* for an aquatic animal goes back to Old English *fisc* ("fish"), which is based on an Indo-European root meaning "fish."

drink like a fish

Many fish swim with their mouths open (to get oxygen by pumping water over their gills) and appear to be constantly drinking water. It is said, then, that to drink a great deal is *to drink like a fish*.

fish

To pull up or out (as the fisherman pulls in a fish) is *to fish*, as in "He had *to fish* a coin out of his pocket." And to seek something indirectly (as the fisherman seeks the fish indirectly with a hook and line, not directly with his hands) is *to fish*, as in "She liked *to fish* for compliments."

fisheye

Fish typically have a fixed, glassy look in their eyes. Therefore, an unfriendly, suspicious look is a *fisheye*.

Among the other objects called a *fisheye* are, in plasterwork, a surface defect having the form of a spot; a gemstone cut too thin for proper brillance; and a type of lens that gives a circular image.

fishing expedition

On a fishing trip, one never knows exactly what one will catch. Therefore, an investigation without a definite purpose and without due regard for proper methods in the hope of gaining information or evidence is a *fishing expedition*.

fish in troubled waters

Fishermen often have their best luck in rough water.

Therefore, to find some personal advantage in a bad situation is *to fish in troubled waters.*

fish or cut bait

On a fishing boat, everyone has to help. If a person is not fishing, he should at least cut bait for the others. On land, the same thing is often true: to make a choice between alternative courses of action is *to fish or cut bait.*

fish out of water

A fish out of water just flops about. It cannot function. Therefore, to be out of one's usual environment, to feel awkward, is to be a *fish out of water.*

fish story

Fishermen are traditionally known for their exaggeration of the size of fish almost caught. Hence, an extravagant or incredible story is a *fish story.*

fishtail

Most fish move their tails from side to side. Therefore, to swerve from side to side, as in a skidding car, is *to fishtail.*

fishy

Anything hard to believe can be called *fishy.* There are two possible reasons for this use of the word. One is that dead fish are noted for their strong odor (generally thought to be repulsive), indicating something of uncertain quality. The other is that most fish, being slippery, are hard to hold—just as a *fishy* story is hard to hold (that is, hard to believe).

kettle of fish

A matter to be considered is a *kettle of fish,* as in "Bestsellers and great books are two different *kettles of fish.*" The expression has evolved from the earlier *pretty kettle of fish* (see *pretty kettle of fish* below).

neither fish nor fowl

In the Middle Ages, each class of people (except the nobility) was associated with a certain kind of food: monks with fish, most people with flesh, and paupers with red (smoked) herring. Food that was not fit for eating by anyone was called *neither fish nor flesh nor good red herring*. Today the expression is usually shortened to *neither fish nor fowl*, and the meaning has broadened from describing food that does not belong to an established class to describing anything that does not belong to a particular class or category.

other fish to fry

To have other important things to do is to have *other fish to fry*.

plenty of other fish in the ocean

A person suffering from unrequited love may be soothed by the reminder that there are many other potential mates in the world. A common way of making that point is to say that there are *plenty of other fish in the ocean* (or *sea*).

pretty kettle of fish

In England, there used to be a popular custom of having outdoor picnics near a river at the start of the salmon run each year. The salmon were snatched out of the river and tossed into a huge kettle of boiling water. Apparently either from the messy appearance of the fish in the kettle or from the messy hands, clothes, and grounds came the general association of those picnics with the idea of confusion and clutter. Therefore, any mess or awkward state of affairs can be called a *pretty* (or *fine* or *nice*) *kettle of fish*, in which *pretty* or *fine* or *nice* is used ironically.

Flea

The Modern English word *flea* for a type of insect goes back to Old English *fleah* ("flea"), which is based on an Indo-European root meaning "flea" and is related to Old English *fleon* ("to flee, run away quickly"). The flea, then, is "the fleeing insect."

flea

Anything small or contemptible can be called a *flea*, as in "He couldn't hurt (or fool) a *flea*."

fleabag

Fleas are often associated with unpleasant or run-down places or things. A cheap hotel, a mangy dog, a worthless racehorse—each of these can be called a *fleabag*.

fleabite

A trifling pain or annoyance is a *fleabite*.

flea-bitten

A horse having a white or gray coat flecked with bay or sorrel is said to be *flea-bitten*.

Something in bad condition is also *flea-bitten*.

flea in one's ear

Since a flea in one's ear would be irritating and painful (as commonly observed with dogs), a stinging rejection or criticism (whether perceived through the ears or not) is a *flea in one's ear*.

Fledgling

The Modern English word *fledgling* for a young bird capable of leaving the nest and surviving comes from the archaic adjective *fledge* ("feathered, fit to fly"), which is based on an Indo-European root meaning "to flow."

fledgling

An immature or inexperienced person or thing is, like a young bird, a *fledgling*.

Fleece

The Modern English word *fleece* for the coat of wool covering a sheep goes back to Old English *fleos* ("fleece"), which is based on an Indo-European root meaning "feather, fleece," which in turn is based on a root meaning "to pluck." Fleece, then, is "that which is plucked off."

fleece

To cut the fleece, or wool, from a sheep is to fleece the

animal. Figuratively, to take something from a person by unfair means is *to fleece* him.

fleecy

Anything resembling the soft, white appearance of fleece can be described as being *fleecy,* as in *"fleecy* clouds."

Fly

The Modern English word *fly* for a type of insect goes back to Old English *fleoge* ("a fly"), which is related to *fleogan* ("to fly"), which is based on an Indo-European root meaning "to move forward, flow." The fly, then, is "the flying insect."

barfly

A heavy drinker, especially one who lingers at bars (as a fly lingers over garbage) or "flies" from bar to bar, is a *barfly.*

fly in the ointment

In the Bible (Ecclesiastes 10:1), there is a passage comparing dead flies in an otherwise good ointment (medicine) to "a little folly" in an otherwise good person. Today any little flaw that ruins what otherwise would be something perfectly good can be called a *fly in the ointment.*

fly on the wall

An unseen witness is sometimes called a *fly on the wall,* as in "I'd love to be a *fly on the wall* to hear what she's saying."

flyspeck

A flyspeck is a spot made by fly excrement. Figuratively, something small and insignificant is a *flyspeck.*

fly trap

The human mouth is jocularly called a *fly trap* (it is not so jocular, of course, when a fly really does wander in).

flyweight

In professional boxing, a fighter weighing from 109 to 112 pounds is called a *flyweight.*

no flies on

Slow-moving animals often tend to attract flies. Alert, active animals, however, can avoid the pests. Thus, it is said of a person who is alert and unlikely to be fooled that there are *no flies on* him.

Fox

The Modern English word *fox* for a type of doglike mammal goes back to Old English *fox* ("fox"), which is based on an Indo-European root meaning "bushy-haired," applied to the fox in reference to its bushy tail.

fox

The fox is noted for its cleverness. To throw pursuing hounds off its scent, the fox will double back on its trail or run into water. A clever, ingenious, or furtive person is called a *fox,* as in "He's a sly *fox."*

To deceive is *to fox.*

fox-trot

Since the late 1800s, *fox-trot* has been the name of a horse gait with short steps in which the hind foot of the animal hits the ground just before the diagonally opposite forefoot. In the early 1900s, *fox-trot* was applied to a type of ballroom dance (some authorities, however, attribute the name of the dance to a dancing master named Fox).

foxy

To be cunning or clever (like a fox) is to be *foxy.*

A physically attractive young woman is described as being *foxy,* perhaps because the fur of a fox is beautiful and valuable.

Frog

The Modern English word *frog* for a type of amphibian goes back to Old English *frogga* ("frog"), which is based on an Indo-European root meaning "to hop, jump." The frog, then, is "the hopper."

frog in the throat

A hoarse voice, which sometimes resembles the sound of a frog, is often called a *frog in the throat.*

leapfrog

From the frog's characteristic hopping, people have invented a game known as *leapfrog*, in which one player bends down and another leaps over him. Any similar type of jump can also be called a *leapfrog*. Figuratively, to move (in any way) ahead of someone or something is *to leapfrog.*

Fur

The Modern English word *fur* for an animal pelt comes from Middle English *furre* ("fur"), a derivative of the verb *furren* ("to cover, line with fur"), which goes back to Old French and Germanic words meaning "sheath, case, lining, covering," all of which are based on an Indo-European root meaning "to cover, protect." Fur, then, is "covering."

make the fur fly

On the American frontier, people probably literally saw the fur fly as animals fought each other, either when the animals fought in the wild or when hunting dogs captured a quarry. Today to cause a disturbance or to do things in a wild hurry is *to make the fur fly.*

Gadfly

The word *gadfly* for a type of insect is a compound of two other English words: *gad* ("spike, bar, rod," especially one used to goad or drive oxen—from Old Norse *gaddr*, "spike, nail, sting") and *fly* ("fly," the insect; see "Fly"). The gadfly, then, is "the goading fly."

gadfly

A gadfly is any one of various kinds of flies that bite or

annoy domestic animals. A person who irritates others with criticism, demands, or ideas is sometimes called a *gadfly*.

Game

The Modern English word *game* for hunted animals goes back to Old English *gamen*. The word originally applied to an amusement. Later, since wild animals were the object of a popular amusement (hunting), the animals themselves came to be called *game*.

fair game

Hunting laws outline well-defined seasons during which certain animals may be killed, that is, it is "fair" to kill them. Therefore, any legitimate object of attack or ridicule is *fair game*.

game

Having a resolute spirit, that is, the spirit of a gamecock, is to be *game*, as in "I'm *game* to enter the haunted house."

Gander

The Modern English word *gander* for a male goose goes back to Old English *gandra* ("gander"), which is based on an Indo-European root meaning "goose."

gander

A dull, stupid person is sometimes called a *gander*.

A gander is noted for its long neck, which appears to be constantly stretching upwards. Thus, from the appearance of a person stretching his neck to look at something, a look or a glance is called a *gander*, as in "Take a *gander* at that."

Gill

The English word *gill* for an organ (in water-breathing animals) through which oxygen is obtained from water probably comes from Old Norse unattested *gil* ("gill," related to Old Norse *giolnar*, "jaws"; notice Modern Swedish *gäl* and Danish *gaelle*, both meaning "gill"), which goes back to an Indo-European root meaning "jaw."

filled to the gills

The gills of a fish are located between its head and its body. The word *gills*, then, is humorously applied to the area just under the human chin or jaws. To exaggerate how stuffed with food or drink a person is, one can say that the person is *filled to the gills.*

green about the gills

As mentioned above (see *filled to the gills*), the word *gills* is sometimes applied to a human. In past centuries, to be *rosy about the gills* was to be in good health; to be *white* (or *blue* or *yellow*) *about the gills* was to be sad or ill; and to be *red in the gills* was to be angry. Today, however, the most common version of this expression is to be *green about* (or *in*) *the gills*, meaning to be ill, especially with nausea brought about by seasickness (the sea, of course, being closely associated with the idea of fish gills).

loaded to the gills

To be drunk is to be *loaded* (or *stewed*) *to the gills.* (For the sense of *loaded* here see *loaded for bear* under "Bear.")

Gnat

The Modern English word *gnat* for a type of small biting fly goes back to Old English *gnaet* ("gnat"), which is based on an Indo-European root meaning "to gnaw." The gnat, then, is "the gnawer."

strain at a gnat and swallow a camel

(See *strain at a gnat and swallow a camel* under "Camel.")

Goat

The Modern English word *goat* for a type of ruminant mammal goes back to Old English *gat* ("goat"), which is based on an Indo-European root meaning "goat."

get one's goat

Formerly, a goat was sometimes stabled with a racehorse to keep the thoroughbred calm. If the goat was stolen just before a race, the horse might get upset and lose the contest. Therefore, to make one angry (that is, to "steal" one's calmness) is *to get one's goat.*

goat

A derogatory term for a man, especially a lecherous one, is *goat.*

Goat is also short for *scapegoat* (see *scapegoat* below).

goatee

A small pointed or tufted beard on a man's chin is called, because of its resemblance to the beard of a he-goat, a *goatee.*

scapegoat

Among the ancient Hebrews, there was an annual Day of Atonement. Two goats were involved in the ritual. One was killed as a sacrifice. The other, after the sins of the people had been symbolically placed on its head, was sent alive into the wilderness. The second goat has been given the name *scapegoat* (because through it the people "escaped" their sins). Today, then, anyone who takes the blame or punishment for others is called a *scapegoat.*

separate the sheep from the goats

In the Bible (Matthew 25:32), there is a passage that describes the Last Judgment: "And before him shall be gathered all nations: and he shall separate them one from another, as a shepherd divideth his sheep from the goats." The sheep are the saved souls; the goats, the lost. Today that idea has broadened, so that to separate those people who have any certain ability or quality from those who do not have that ability or quality is *to separate the sheep from the goats.*

Goose

The Modern English word *goose* for a type of waterfowl goes back to Old English *gos* ("goose"), which is based on an Indo-European root meaning "goose."

cook one's goose

To cook one's goose means to frustrate or ruin one's plans. A famous early use of this expression was in a London street song of 1851. In that year, the pope tried to reestablish the Catholic hierarchy in England through the appointment of Cardinal Wiseman. Some of the English who were against the idea made up a song, part of which went like this: "If they come here we'll cook their goose,/The Pope and Cardinal Wiseman."

However, the expression *to cook one's goose* was already well known before 1851. There are at least three theories about its origin. One theory relates to an old story that several hundred years ago the people of a besieged town hung a goose (as a symbol of stupidity, hence as an insult to the besiegers) in a tower to show their contempt for the enemy outside the gates. The enemy then burned (or threatened to burn) the entire town, thus cooking the goose. In this way, the cooked goose became a symbol of defeat.

Another theory is that the expression is a reference to the fable about the goose that laid the golden eggs. *To cook one's goose* would be to cut off one's source of income, to halt one's plans.

However, the most likely source for the expression may be the English custom of eating a goose at Christmas. Such a goose would be raised or purchased with great care and high hopes. To steal one's goose and cook it would be to frustrate one's holiday plans.

gone goose

A person in a hopeless situation is, like the bird plucked for dinner, a *gone goose*.

goose

The goose is generally thought to be a stupid bird. A foolish person, therefore, is sometimes called a *goose*, as in the lighthearted "silly *goose*."

goose egg

(See *lay an egg* under "Egg.")

gooseflesh

Through cold or fear, people sometimes develop a rough

condition of the skin. This skin, because it resembles that of a plucked goose, is called *gooseflesh* (or *goose bumps, goose pimples, gooseskin*).

the goose hangs high

The goose hangs high means all is well. The origin of this expression is uncertain. One theory is that the phrase refers to the belief that geese fly higher when the weather is mild than they do when it is wet or threatening; thus, the image of a high-flying (or "hanging") goose symbolizes good weather and, by extension, any good condition. Another theory is that *the goose hangs high* refers to the old custom of hanging a goose above the sign of an inn where that desirable bird was on the menu; thus, the image of a high-hanging goose symbolized good food and, by extension, any good condition.

gooseneck

Any curved object (such as the shaft of a type of lamp) that resembles the neck of a goose can be called a *gooseneck*.

goose step

The troops of some armies march with a step in which the legs are swung high and kept straight and stiff. The step brings to mind the waddle of a goose and is therefore called the *goose step*.

kill the goose that laid the golden eggs

(See *kill the goose that laid the golden eggs* under "Egg.")

wild-goose chase

In England, about the year 1600, there was a popular game played on horseback. The leader followed any course he chose while one or more others trailed at steady intervals from each other. The movement of the leader and the followers reminded people of the flight of geese, so the game was called a *wild-goose chase*.

Wild-goose chase soon came to mean any kind of strange, changeable course of action taken by one person and perhaps followed by others.

Later the game disappeared. New generations of people, however, continued to use the catchy phrase *wild-goose chase*. But they gave it a new meaning (the original one, the game, being completely forgotten): a pursuit of something as unlikely to be caught as a wild goose. Today any hopeless quest is a *wild-goose chase*.

Gorilla

The English word *gorilla* for a type of ape is actually a New Latin word (first used for the ape in 1847) derived from Greek *gorillai* (first recorded in the fifth or sixth century B.C.), which is a Greek version of a native African name of a tribe of hairy people.

gorilla

While it is said to be basically shy and friendly unless provoked, the gorilla nevertheless has long had a popular reputation for fierceness. Therefore, a coarse, cruel (and usually ugly) man is sometimes referred to as a *gorilla*.

Grub

The English word *grub* for a wormlike larva of an insect comes from the verb *to grub*, which goes back to an Indo-European root meaning "to dig." The grub, then, is "the digger."

grub

The noun (insect) and verb (to dig up) meanings of *grub* have intermixed, so that some extended senses combine both ideas. For example, a drudge or a slovenly person is a *grub*.

grubby

Grubby literally means infested with grubs. By extension, *grubby* means dirty, slovenly, or contemptible.

Guinea Pig

No one is certain how the guinea pig (which is really a

rodent, not a pig) got its name. However, the animal is probably named after "Guineamen," traders who typically traveled from England to Guinea (in West Africa) to South America and then back to England. It was in South America, not Guinea, that the Guineamen actually picked up the animal. Since a region in northwest South America is called Guiana, some authorities have speculated that when the sailors took the rodent back to England, folk etymology transformed *Guiana* into the more familiar *Guinea* in the naming of the animal.

guinea pig

Guinea pigs are often used in scientific experiments. Therefore, the subject of any kind of experiment can be called a *guinea pig*.

Hackle

Hackles are the long feathers on the neck of a bird (especially a domestic rooster) or the erectile hairs at the back of the neck of any of various animals (such as a dog). The Modern English word *hackle* comes from Middle English *hakell* ("hatchel" [a flaxcomb with long hooklike teeth] or "feathers on the neck of a bird"), which is based on an Indo-European root meaning "hook."

get one's hackles up

The hackles of some animals rise when the animals are angry. Figuratively, among humans, to be aroused or ready to fight is *to get one's hackles up*.

Hackney

The Modern English word *hackney* for a type of horse comes from Middle English *hakeney* ("hackney"), which probably comes from *Hakeney* (the name of an English village where hackney horses were raised, now *Hackney*, a borough of London).

hack

(See *hackney* below.)

hackney

The hackney is a breed of horse developed in England specifically for the purpose of ordinary riding, as distinguished from a war horse, a draft horse, and so on. Early in its history, the hackney became well known as a horse let out for hire. *Hackney* meaning a horse kept for hire is now obsolete (replaced by *hack*, short for *hackney*), but by extension *hackney* now means a carriage or an automobile kept for hire.

The shortened form of *hack*, besides meaning a horse kept for hire, has such extensions as a worn-out horse, a taxicab, and one who forfeits professional integrity for wages to do routine work (used especially of writers).

hackneyed

The adjective *hackneyed* originally meant hired (now obsolete). The word has extended to its present sense of trite or stale, in reference to a horse or other entity used (hired) so frequently that it has lost its freshness.

Halcyon

The English word *halcyon* for the kingfisher (a type of bird) comes from Latin *(h)alcyon* ("kingfisher"), which comes from Greek *(h)alkyon* ("kingfisher"). The correct Greek form was *alkyon*, but the *h* was commonly added under the influence of Greek *hals* ("sea").

halcyon

In an ancient legend, a bird called a halcyon (usually identified with the kingfisher) is said to nest at sea about the time of the winter solstice and to have the power to charm the wind and the waves into calmness. Because the bird is able to produce a desirable condition for itself, *halcyon* has come to have the adjectival meanings of calm, peaceful, prosperous, happy, carefree; the word is commonly used in the expression *halcyon days*, meaning a period of peace and tranquillity.

Hare

The Modern English word *hare* for a type of long-eared mammal goes back to Old English *hara* ("hare"), which is based on an Indo-European root meaning "gray." The hare, then, is named for its typically light gray color.

hare and hounds

Hare and hounds is a game in which certain players, the hares, begin by taking off on a long run. As they run, they scatter pieces of paper, called the scent. Other players, the hounds, follow the paper trail and try to catch the hares before the hares reach a certain point. The name of the game is, of course, derived from the analogy with real hares and hounds. (The game is also known as a paper chase.)

harebrained

To be foolish or reckless (that is, to have no more brains than a hare) is to be *harebrained*. The idea of a hare being foolish or reckless probably comes from the earlier expression *(as) mad as a March hare* (see *mad as a March hare* below).

harelip

A condition in which the human upper lip is split like that of a hare is called a *harelip*.

mad as a March hare

In March, male hares establish a breeding hierarchy by fighting each other. They kick, jump up and down, twist their bodies in midair, and box with their forepaws. From this wild behavior has come the idea that to leap and jump about crazily is to be *(as) mad* (meaning crazy) *as a March hare.*

Hawk

The Modern English word *hawk* for a type of bird goes back to Old English *h(e)afoc* ("hawk"), which is based on an Indo-European root meaning "to seize." The hawk, then, is "the seizer," so called because of the way the bird attacks its prey.

hawk

The hawk is a bird of prey. A person who preys on (cheats) others is sometimes called a *hawk.*

A person who prefers fighting rather than talking (especially in international conflicts) is called a *hawk.* (Contrast *dove* under "Dove.")

The hawk is known for its keen vision. A person with sharp eyesight is sometimes compared to a hawk, as in "He watched her like a *hawk.*"

hawk-eyed

To have keen vision is to be *hawk-eyed.*

Hen

The Modern English word *hen* for the female of various animals goes back to Old English *henn* ("hen"), which is the feminine of *hana* ("rooster"), which is based on an Indo-European root meaning "to sing, crow." The hen, then, derives its name from the rooster's being a "singer."

hen

A woman—especially a fussy middle-aged one—is sometimes called a *hen.*

henpeck

It is said that a hen occasionally pecks at a rooster's feathers. That idea is sometimes applied to a human wife and husband, so that for a wife to domineer over her husband is for her *to henpeck* him.

mad as a wet hen

A hen does not actually seem to get particularly angry when wet. Nevertheless, a person who is angry is often said to be *(as) mad as a wet hen.*

mother hen

A protective woman, being compared to a hen that covers its frightened chicks with its wings, is called a *mother hen.*

Herring

The Modern English word *herring* for a type of fish goes back to Old English *haering* ("herring"), which may be based (like *hare*) on an Indo-European root meaning "gray." The herring, then, would be "the gray fish."

dead as a herring

(As) dead as a doornail means certainly dead. Many variants of this expression have been coined. One is *(as) dead as a herring*, a fish being selected for the phrase because its smell emphasizes decay, and the herring being chosen as the specific fish simply because it is so common. (See *dead as a dodo* under "Dodo" and *dead as a mackerel* under "Mackerel" for similar expressions.)

neither fish nor flesh nor good red herring

(See *neither fish nor fowl* under "Fish.")

red herring

In England, dog trainers used to draw red (smoked) herring across the trail of a fox to destroy or confuse the scent. Then hunting dogs were set to the trail. The smell of the red herring tested and sharpened the ability of the hounds to stay with the trail of the fox. Today anything that takes one's attention away from the real issue can be called a *red herring*.

Hide

The Modern English word *hide* for an animal skin goes back to Old English *hyd* ("hide"), which is based on an Indo-European root meaning "to cover." A hide, then, is literally "a covering."

hide

The skin of a human being is sometimes referred to as a *hide*. The word has extended its meaning to include the idea of safety or welfare, as in "The only thing he cares about is his own *hide*."

hidebound

Of underfed cattle it is said that to have the hide clinging closely to the back and ribs is to be hidebound. Figuratively transferred to humans, *hidebound* means narrow and rigid in opinion.

hide nor hair

A trace or evidence of someone or something is commonly expressed in the phrase *hide nor* (or *or*) *hair,* as in "They found neither *hide nor hair* of the missing car."

tan one's hide

In the tanning process, an animal hide is toughened into leather. Figuratively, to thrash one (presumably resulting in the toughening of the skin) is *to tan one's hide.*

Hog

The Modern English word *hog* for a swine comes from Old English *hogg* ("hog"). The original meaning of the word is uncertain. Some authorities say that *hog* is related to English dialectal *hag* ("to cut") and Old Norse *hoggva* ("to cut"), referring to the castration of the male. Others say that *hog* goes back to a Celtic word meaning "swine," which is based on an Indo-European root meaning "pig."

go hog-wild

To become wildly excited is (presumably like a wild hog) *to go hog-wild.*

go whole hog

To go (the) whole hog means to go all the way, to do completely. There are two theories about the origin of this expression.

One theory is related to the fact that in England a shilling (a unit of money) was once called a *hog,* while in the United States a ten-cent piece was given the same nickname. To spend the whole hog at one time would have been *to go (the) whole hog.* From spending completely, the idea could have broadened to mean doing anything completely.

Another theory about the origin of *to go (the) whole hog* is related to a poem by the English poet William Cowper ("The Love of the World Reproved; or, Hypocrisy Detected," 1779). The poem explains that Mohammed had forbidden Moslems to eat a certain part of the hog, but the Moslems could not agree on which part was forbidden. So each Moslem ate what he wanted and left some part he did not like. The result was that the Moslems, as a group, ended up eating the whole hog. From eating completely, the idea could have broadened to mean doing anything completely.

hog

The hog has a reputation for being filthy and greedy. A coarse, dirty, selfish, or gluttonous person is sometimes called a *hog*.

To take more than one's due is *to hog*.

hogshead

A large cask or barrel, especially one containing from 63 to 140 gallons, has long been referred to as a *hogshead*. It is uncertain why the name was originally used, unless the shape of the container centuries ago reminded people of a hog's head.

hogtie

To hogtie a hog is to tie it with all four feet together. To tie a human's limbs together is also *to hogtie*. That idea has broadened, so that to make helpless in any way is *to hogtie*.

hogwash

Hogwash is the kitchen garbage given to hogs. Therefore, any worthless or meaningless matter can be called *hogwash*.

independent as a hog on ice, like a hog on ice

(As) independent as a hog on ice and *like a hog on ice* are American expressions originating in the nineteenth century. The second phrase means awkward(ly) or inse-cure(ly), in a manner to be expected from a hog literally sliding about on ice.

(As) independent as a hog on ice, however, is an intensive meaning quite independent. The origin of this expression is uncertain. Many theories have been proposed. One theory is that a hog on ice might crouch down and be afraid to move. It would refuse help and therefore appear to be independent. This origin seems unlikely because it directly conflicts with the popular impression of a hog on ice as revealed in the expression *like a hog on ice.*

Another theory is related to the fact that in the Scottish game of curling, the stone pushed over the ice is called a *hog.* If a *hog* (stone) got stuck in the ice, the stone would not budge. It would therefore be an "independent" *hog* on the ice. One problem with this theory is that the expression *(as) independent as a hog on ice* does not actually appear in Scotland itself.

Perhaps the most likely origin is that the expression is a reference to a hog that has been slaughtered and packed whole on ice for preservation. The hog would appear indifferent or "independent." The *Oxford English Dictionary's* earliest record of *(as) independent as a hog on ice* is from 1857 in San Francisco, California. And ice was first shipped to California from the East during the Gold Rush, just a few years before the expression was recorded. Preserving food with ice was a novelty in the region and was therefore perfectly likely to spark a figure of speech.

live high off the hog

The most tender and expensive cuts of meat from a hog are high on the animal's body. To eat the high parts of a hog is to eat well. Therefore, figuratively, to live well, especially with plenty of money and material goods, is *to live* (or *eat*) *high off the hog.*

roadhog

A *roadhog* is a selfish driver who *hogs* the road. (See *hog* above.)

Honey

The Modern English word *honey* for a fluid produced by

bees goes back to Old English *hunig* ("honey"), which is based on an Indo-European root meaning "yellow, golden." Honey, then, is "yellow substance."

honey

Any sweet substance can be called, like the bee fluid, *honey.* Sweetness itself, literally or figuratively (as in a quality of voice), is *honey. Honey* is also a term of endearment, meaning sweet one.

In slang, something especially fine is a *honey.*

To sweeten as if with honey or to cajole with sweet talk is *to honey.*

honeycomb

A honeycomb is a structure constructed from beeswax by honeybees. It holds honey and eggs. The honeycomb is built in hexagonal, thin-walled cells. Anything suggesting such a structure, especially by containing many small units or holes, is a *honeycomb.*

To fill with holes, literally (as in "The wood was *honeycombed* with ant burrows") or figuratively (as in "The story was *honeycombed* with lies"), is *to honeycomb.*

honeymoon

A trip taken by a newly married couple or any initial period of harmony is called a *honeymoon. Honey,* of course, here refers to the pleasure and the sweetness of the relationship. *Moon* originally may have compared the mutual affection of a newly married couple to the changing moon, which is no sooner full than it begins to wane. Today, however, *moon* is commonly taken to refer to the period of a month.

Hoof

The Modern English word *hoof* for a horny covering of the digits in certain animals goes back to Old English *hof* ("hoof"), which is based on an Indo-European root meaning "hoof."

hoof, hoofer, hoof it

The human foot is sometimes informally called a *hoof*.
Dancing, of course, involves the use of one's feet, or
hooves. Therefore, to dance is *to hoof*, and a dancer is a *hoofer*.

To walk (since walking, like dancing, involves one's feet,
or *hooves*) is sometimes expressed as *to hoof it*.

Horn

The Modern English word *horn* for a bony projection on
the head of an animal comes from Old English *horn* ("horn"),
which is based on an Indo-European root meaning "the
uppermost part of the body."

greenhorn

The adjective *green* has long been used to mean unripe or
young, as in reference to fruits or vegetables. *Greenhorn*,
then, was originally applied to an ox with "green," or young,
horns. That sense of *greenhorn* is now obsolete. But today an
inexperienced person or a person who is unacquainted with
local customs is a *greenhorn*.

horn

People in ancient times often made musical instruments
from animal horns. The instruments themselves were also
called *horns*. Today the word *horn* is applied to many kinds of
wind instruments, most commonly the "French *horn*."

horn in

To push oneself forward boldly or to interrupt (like a
bull rushing forward with his horns) is *to horn in*.

lock horns

Animals with horns, such as the male moose, sometimes
battle each other fiercely, banging and locking their horns.
Among angry humans, then, to disagree or conflict violently is *to lock horns*.

on the horns of a dilemma

No one would welcome the idea of sitting on either one

of the two pointed horns of an animal. In any situation, to have to choose between two equally bad alternatives is to be *on the horns of a dilemma.*

pull in one's horns

When disturbed, a snail will pull in its hornlike tentacles (which contain its eyes). Therefore, to retreat or restrain oneself is *to pull* (or *draw*) *in one's horns.*

take the bull by the horns

(See *take the bull by the horns* under "Bull.")

Hornet

The Modern English word *hornet* for a type of insect goes back to Old English *hyrnet* ("hornet"), which is influenced by the word *horn*, in reference to the hornet's hornlike antennae.

hornet's nest

The hornet, a member of the wasp family, can inflict a serious sting. A nest of hornets is a mean enemy when aroused. Among humans, any dangerous situation or angry reaction can be called a *hornet's nest.*

mad as a hornet

The hornet is popularly associated with angry attacks and painful stings. Thus, to be extremely angry is to be *(as) mad as a hornet.*

Horse

The Modern English word *horse* for a type of mammal goes back to Old English *hors* ("horse"), which has a Germanic origin. The ultimate source is uncertain, but *horse* may be based on an Indo-European root meaning "to run" or "to jump." The horse, then, would be "the running animal" or "the jumping animal."

back the wrong horse

From betting on a losing horse in a horserace comes the

idea that to be wrong in any kind of judgment is *to back the wrong horse.*

beat a dead horse

To try to get any action out of a dead horse by beating it would, of course, be useless. Similarly, to try to bring back any topic or idea that appears to be hopeless is *to beat* (or *flog*) *a dead horse.*

change horses in midstream

To try to change horses in the middle of a stream would be extremely dangerous. That idea has been applied to humans: to risk a disruption in policy by changing leaders in the middle of a crisis is *to change* (or *swap*) *horses in midstream* (or *while crossing a stream*). Apparently Abraham Lincoln first popularized this expression when he used a variant of it in his reelection year of 1864, his purpose being to say that his supporters had evidently concluded that it would be dangerous to change leaders in the middle of the Civil War crisis. Today the expression has developed a broader meaning: to change one's ideas or plans in the middle of a project is *to change* (or *swap*) *horses in midstream* (or *while crossing a stream*).

charley horse

A *charley horse* is a cramp or a stiffness in a muscle, especially in the arm or the leg. The origin of this expression is uncertain. But *Charley* was once a name for a night watchman, probably so named after Charles I of England (1600-49), who expanded the watch system, or after Charles II (1630-85), who gave many watchman jobs to disabled veterans. Probably from its application to lame watchmen, *Charley* became a common name for old lame horses. By the late 1800s, *charley horse* was used for a stiff, sore muscle itself, especially among baseball players.

dark horse

A racehorse whose abilities are unknown has long been referred to as a dark horse. The term *dark horse* originated in a novel (*The Young Duke*, 1831) by the British author-statesman Benjamin Disraeli: "A dark horse, which had never been thought of . . . rushed past the grand stand in sweeping triumph." Now, in any kind of contest, a little-known competitor, especially one who does unexpectedly well, can be called a *dark horse.*

eat like a horse

To eat heavily is *to eat like a horse.*

from the horse's mouth

The age of a horse can be determined by checking the number and the condition of its teeth. Someone trying to sell a horse might claim that it is younger than it really is. A smart buyer, however, will look into the horse's mouth to determine the animal's true age. The horse's own mouth is the most reliable source of information. That idea has broadened, so that any information from an original or reliable source is said to be *from the horse's mouth.*

high horse

In the Middle Ages, a "high" horse was a heavy charger used in battles and tournaments. At public gatherings, such a horse was a sign that the rider was a person of importance. If a person tried to act more important than he really was, he was, figuratively, mounting a *high horse.* Today any conceited attitude is a *high horse.* To reverse this conceited attitude—that is, to become less arrogant—is *to come* (or *get*) *off one's high horse.*

hobby, hobbyhorse, ride a hobbyhorse

In England, a small horse was formerly called a *hobby* or a *hobbyhorse* (*hobby* coming from Middle English *hoby, hobyn,* which come from *Hobby, Hobin,* which are nicknames of *Robbie, Robin, Robert*). Extended, *hobbyhorse* has been applied to a lightweight figure of a horse fastened to the waist of a dancer, as in the morris dance or in Spanish dance rituals. A child's toy consisting of a long stick with an imitation horse's head on the end is a *hobbyhorse* (also called *stick horse*), as is an imitation horse on a merry-go-round. A *rocking horse* (see *rocking horse* below) is sometimes called a *hobbyhorse.*

A pursuit engaged in for relaxation has been compared to the riding of a toy horse and is therefore called a *hobby* (short for *hobbyhorse*).

Figuratively, something, such as an idea, that preoccupies one is a *hobbyhorse*. And to obsessively pursue a single object or idea is, like a child on a toy horse, *to ride a hobbyhorse*.

hold one's horses

To control one's own impulses, like a rider holding the reins of a team of horses to control the animals, is *to hold one's horses*.

horse-and-buggy

Since a horse-drawn buggy is no longer a standard means of transportation, *horse-and-buggy* has come to mean clinging to outdated attitudes, as in *"horse-and-buggy* thinking."

horse around

To engage in horseplay (see *horseplay* below) is *to horse around*.

horse collar, horse-collar

A horse collar is part of the harness, by which a horse is controlled. The idea of controlling has extended to baseball, in which *horse collar* means a zero or a lack of success, as in "to go for the *horse collar*" and "to wear the *horse collar*."

To horse-collar, said of a pitcher, is to hold (an opposing batter) hitless or (an opposing team) runless.

horsefeathers

Horsefeathers means nonsense. The origin of this expression is uncertain. Most slanguists prefer to see it as simply a euphemism for its scatological cousin. Perhaps it is. But why *feathers*? The probable answer is that there really are fringes of long hair on a horse's body, such as those on the forehead, that are called *feathers* and are regarded as natural ornaments. However, in the popular mind, a horse with "feathers" seems incongruous or nonsensical. Thus, *horsefeathers* has come to mean nonsense.

horse latitudes

The *horse latitudes* are either of two belts of latitudes located over the oceans at about 30 degrees north or south and characterized by high pressure, calms, and light changeable winds. The expression refers to the fact that Old World ships carrying horses to America were often becalmed in those latitudes for long periods of time, thus running low on fresh water and having to dispose of their horse cargos.

horselaugh

When a horse neighs, it pulls back its lips and appears to give a sarcastic smile. From the sound and the appearance of the horse's neigh comes the idea that a loud, coarse human laugh (especially a sneering one) can be called a *horselaugh*.

horse of another color

Formerly, *horse of the same* (or *that*) *color* meant that two or more things were alike in some way. (*Birds of a feather* was formed in a similar manner.) Gradually, though, the emphasis has changed to the negative, so that one thing entirely different from another is a *horse of another* (or *different*) *color*.

horse opera

An opera is a musical play, generally noted for its seriousness. A television play or a motion picture about the American Wild West is called, because it has horses and because it usually takes its subject seriously, a *horse opera*. The name also has an ironic implication in that the musical opera is popularly regarded in America as being pompous and fancy, while the *horse opera* is the opposite—folksy and simple.

horseplay

Horses are noted for their wild romps when they feel frisky. Among humans, any rough, noisy, unrestrained play is called *horseplay*.

horsepower

Horsepower is the rate of power that a horse exerts in pulling. In machinery, a certain conventional unit of power is called a *horsepower*.

horse sense

Practical common sense is *horse sense*, the kind of sense needed in a *horse trade* (see *horse trade* below).

horse trade

Before automobiles were invented, horses provided people with the main means of traveling. Therefore, horses were bought, sold, and traded on a wide scale. Horse trading sometimes developed into quite a complicated affair, involving much shrewd bargaining. Today any give-and-take bargaining can be called a *horse trade*.

if wishes were horses, beggars would ride

A proverbial way of saying that a certain thing, though desired, is unlikely to come about is *if wishes were horses, beggars would ride*.

iron horse

Because it is powerful and because it originally competed with the horse as a means of traveling and hauling, a locomotive engine has been called an *iron horse*.

lock the barn door after the horse has been stolen

To take precautionary measures too late is *to lock the barn door after the horse has been stolen* (or *has run away*). This is an Americanized version of an expression that is common in many languages and comes in many variants. In England, *stable* or *stable door* is generally used instead of *barn door*.

long horse

Because of its general horselike shape, a certain apparatus in gymnastics is called a *long horse*.

look a gift horse in the mouth

As mentioned above (see *from the horse's mouth*), the age of a horse can be determined by checking its teeth. It would obviously be rude for a person to open the mouth of a horse he has just received as a gift and to begin to check the animal's age and value. In general, then, to be critical in any way of a gift of any kind is *to look a gift horse in the mouth*.

one-horse

Any vehicle drawn by a single horse must be fairly small. Therefore, anything thought to be small and unimportant can be described as *one-horse*, as in *"one-horse town."*

the Pale Horse

The Pale Horse is death. The source of the expression is a biblical passage (Revelation 6:8): "And I looked, and behold, a pale horse: and his name that sat on him was Death."

put the cart before the horse

To pull a cart, a horse must naturally be stationed in front of the vehicle. To put the cart in front of the horse would be to reverse the natural or practical way of doing things. Therefore, in general, to get the order of things mixed up is *to put* (or *set*) *the cart before the horse*.

rocking horse

An imitation horse made so that a child can sit and rock on it is called a *rocking horse*.

sawhorse

A sawbuck (see *sawbuck* under "Buck") is often called a *sawhorse*.

side horse

Because of its general horselike shape, a certain apparatus in gymnastics is called a *side horse*.

stalking-horse

A horse or a horse-shaped portable screen behind which a hunter hides himself while stalking (hunting) game is called a stalking-horse. Thus, a *stalking-horse* is anything that hides a true purpose. In politics, for example, a candidate put forward to hide the real candidacy of someone else is a *stalking-horse.*

strong as a horse

To be very strong is to be *(as) strong as a horse.*

Trojan horse

During the Trojan War, Greeks hid in a large wooden horse, gained entrance to Troy, and later opened the gates to their army; thus the Greeks conquered the Trojans. Today someone or something that subverts from within is a *Trojan horse.*

workhorse, work like a horse

To work very hard is *to work like a horse.* A person who thus works is a *workhorse.*

you can lead a horse to water, but you can't make it drink

You can lead a horse to water, but you can't make it drink means you can show someone a solution to a problem, but you cannot force him to accept it.

Hound

The Modern English word *hound* for a dog (especially a hunting dog) goes back to Old English *hund* ("hound"), which is based on an Indo-European root meaning "dog."

bloodhound

A bloodhound is a large keen-scented dog that was once widely used for tracking large game. A person who keenly pursues is a *bloodhound.* In particular, a detective is a *bloodhound.*

chowhound

A hungry hound typically gulps down its food as fast as possible. Among humans, a person extremely fond of food is a *chowhound.*

hare and hounds

(See *hare and hounds* under "Hare.")

hound

Hound, like *dog*, is a name sometimes given to a disliked person.

A hound (hunting dog) is trained to pursue animals. Therefore, to pursue or bother anyone is *to hound* him.

Ivory

The English word *ivory* for the material forming the tusk of an elephant goes back to Latin *eboreus* ("of ivory"), which is based on *ebur* ("ivory"), which is probably of Egyptian origin (compare Egyptian *abu*, "ivory").

ivory

Something that is, or was formerly, made of ivory or that suggests ivory is called an *ivory*, usually in the plural *ivories*, such as piano keys, dice, and human teeth. A creamy shade of white is called *ivory*.

Jackal

The English word *jackal* for a type of wild dog comes from Turkish *chakal* ("jackal"), which in turn goes back through Persian *shagal* ("jackal") to ancient Sanskrit *srgala* ("jackal," literally "the howler"). When English speakers adapted Turkish *chakal*, they changed the *chak* to *jack*. In English, *jack* ("male" or "small") is a common addition to the names of many animals, as in *jackass*, *jackdaw*, and *jackrabbit*. Since a jackal is about the size of a fox, the *jack* in its name is perhaps originally "small." But, more likely, English speakers changed *chak* to *jack* simply because the latter form was already familiar to them as an animal name.

jackal

At one time, it was believed that the jackal hunted prey

for the lion, which then came along and took the meat. Among humans, one who does degrading or dishonest jobs for someone else is called a *jackal*.

Jackass

The word *jackass* for a horselike mammal comes from two other English words: *jack* ("male") and *ass* ("ass, donkey"), the jackass being a male ass.

jackass

The word *jackass*, like the words *ass* and *donkey*, is often used to name a foolish person.

Jade

The English word *jade* for a worn-out horse comes from Old Norse *jalda* ("mare").

jade

Jade is a contemptuous name for a broken-down, vicious, or worthless horse. A disreputable woman is sometimes called a *jade*.

jaded

Because of the characteristics of a jade (horse), a person who is exhausted or dissipated or dulled by excess can be described as being *jaded*.

Jay

The English word *jay* for a family of birds goes back to Late Latin *gaius* ("jay"), which is probably originally an attempt to imitate the bird's cry but is influenced in spelling by the Latin personal name *Gaius*.

jay

Some jays, such as the common blue jay, are noted for mingling melodious whistles with harsh shrieks and for mimicking the calls of other birds. Therefore, among humans, a noisy chatterbox is a *jay*. Jays are also noted for their brightly colored feathers. So a gaudily dressed person is a *jay.* A naive, countrified person (that is, one who lives, or might as well live, among the backwoods blue jays) is a *jay.*

jayhawker

A *jayhawker* was a member of the Kansas bands of anti-slavery guerrillas who performed raids on Missouri before and during the Civil War. The term has since become a nickname for any Kansan.

To jayhawk, a back-formation from *jayhawker,* means to raid.

The origin of *jayhawker* is uncertain. According to one theory, the expression refers to a fictitious bird, the jayhawk, which would combine the thieving qualities of the jay and the ferocious qualities of the hawk. Some sources say that the term was first used in Australia (to mean bandit, plunderer, murderer) and entered the United States through the many Australians who migrated to California during the Gold Rush in the 1840s and 1850s.

jaywalk

From *jay* meaning a stupid or countrified person comes the verb *to jaywalk,* meaning to walk carelessly across streets in an unsafe manner.

naked as a jaybird

Many kinds of birds are born covered with down (small, soft feathers). But a few, such as the blue jay, are naked when hatched. Therefore, someone without clothes on is said to be *(as) naked as a jaybird.*

Jellyfish

The jellyfish is so named because of its jellylike body.

jellyfish

The jellyfish does not have a fixed form. The shape of its body keeps changing as the bouncing water pushes it about. A person, therefore, who cannot make or keep strong decisions is a *jellyfish.*

Kangaroo

The English word *kangaroo* is adopted from the Australian native name for the animal, which is based on the Australian Aboriginal verb *kanga* ("to leap, jump"). The kangaroo, then, is "the jumper."

kangaroo court

Apparently because of the kangaroo's characteristic jumping, a mock court in which the principles of law and justice are disregarded or perverted (that is, "jumped" over) is called a *kangaroo court*.

Kid

The English word *kid* for a young goat goes back to Old Norse *kith* ("kid"), which is perhaps originally an attempt to imitate the sound of the animal.

kid

The word *kid* has long meant a young goat. Today it also means a young person.

To tease someone (that is, to make a kid—meaning goat or fool—of him) is *to kid* him.

kid-glove, with kid gloves

Kid gloves are dress gloves made of kid leather. The adjective *kid-glove* means marked by extreme care, as if with delicate gloves on. To treat with special consideration or in a tactful manner is to treat *with kid gloves*.

Kite

The Modern English word *kite* for a type of bird of prey goes back to Old English *cyta* ("kite"), which is based on an Indo-European imitative root meaning "to scream." The kite, then, is named for its cry.

go fly a kite

A slang expression meaning get lost or go jump in(to) a lake is *go fly a kite*. (See *kite*, second paragraph, below.)

high as a kite

To be very drunk is to be *(as) high as a kite*. (See *kite*, second paragraph, below.)

kite

A kite is a type of hawk, a bird of prey. Thus, a person who preys on others is sometimes called a *kite*.

The kite is noted for its graceful flight and for its habit of hovering in the air. Hence, a lightweight device flown in the wind on the end of a string is called a *kite*.

A bad check used to raise or keep credit is called, in a figurative reference to the flying device, a *kite*.

kites

The highest sails on a ship, used in a light breeze, are called *kites*.

Kitten

The English word *kitten* for the young of various animals is a blend of English *kitling* ("kitten," from Old Norse *ketlinger*, "kitten") and Old North French *caton* ("little cat," from Old North French *cat*, "cat," which comes from Late Latin *cattus*, "cat").

have kittens

To lose one's composure is *to have kittens*. This expression is generally regarded as twentieth-century American slang. But it had precursors. In 1618 was recorded this quotation: "Your mother's cat has kittened in your mouth." And in 1883: "The cat has kittened," meaning something has happened.

kitten

The word *kitten*, applied originally to the young of the cat and to the young of certain other small mammals, is today often applied as a term of endearment to a young girl.

kittenish

A kitten is noted for its cute, shy playfulness. A person who acts the same way is often described as being *kittenish*.

weak as a kitten

A kitten is typically weak, fragile, and wobbly. Among humans, to be extremely weak is to be *(as) weak as a kitten*.

Lamb

The Modern English word *lamb* for the young of the sheep goes back to Old English *lamb* ("lamb"), which may be based on an Indo-European root meaning "brown" (compare *bear* and *beaver*, which also have a root meaning "brown" but which come from a different Indo-European source).

lamb

The lamb is known for its gentle manner. A gentle, timid, innocent person is sometimes called a *lamb*.

However, such an innocent, trusting person is exactly the type who can easily be fooled by a cheater. Therefore, one who is easily cheated is a *lamb*.

Lamb is also used as a simple term of endearment.

two shakes of a lamb's tail

The word *shake* has long been used to represent a brief period of time. Long ago, people used such expressions as *in the shake of a hand*, *wait a shake*, and *in two shakes*. The shakes referred to could be of any kind, but they probably referred most often to shakes of a hand or of a dice box. Today to do something in a short time is to do it in *two shakes of a lamb's tail*. A lamb's tail is used in the expression probably because it really does move faster than the tails of most other animals.

Lark

The Modern English word *lark* for a type of bird goes back to Old English *lawerce* ("lark"), which is of uncertain origin, though it has been suggested that the name may be imitative of the bird's cry.

happy as a lark

Because of the lark's cheery early-morning song, to be joyful is to be *(as) happy as a lark.*

sing like a lark

To sing beautifully is *to sing like a lark.*

up with the lark

The lark's early-morning song is the source of yet another expression: to be up early is to be *up with the lark.*

Leech

The Modern English word *leech* for a type of bloodsucking worm goes back to Old English *laece* ("leech"), which is a transferred use of *laece* ("physician"). The worm is so named because physicians formerly used one species of the bloodsucker to bleed their patients.

Some early spellings of the word for the worm (such as Old English *lyce,* Middle English *liche,* and Middle Dutch *lieke*) suggest that it may originally have been a separate word that took on the spelling of *laece/leech* ("physician") through folk etymology.

leech

Since the leech is a bloodsucking parasite, any person who takes a great deal of value from another without giving something in return can be called a *leech.*

Leviathan

In several places in the Old Testament is mentioned a monstrous sea animal (real or imagined) that often symbolizes evil. The English word for that creature is *leviathan,* which is adopted from Late Latin *leviathan,* itself from Hebrew *liwyathan,* which is of uncertain origin but may be related to Arabic *liyatu* ("snake").

leviathan

Any large animal (especially a sea animal) can, in reference to the biblical sea creature, be called a *leviathan*. The word has further extended, so that anything unusually large or formidable for its kind is a *leviathan*. Because of the book *Leviathan* (1651) by Thomas Hobbes, a political state, especially a totalitarian one, is called a *Leviathan* or a *Leviathan State*.

Limpet

The Modern English word *limpet* for a type of mollusk goes back to Old English *lempedu* ("limpet"), which comes from Medieval Latin *lampreda* ("lamprey, limpet"), itself a blend of Latin *naupreda* ("mud-lamprey, limpet") and Latin *lambere* ("to lick"). *Lambere* ultimately goes back to an Indo-European imitative root meaning "to lick up," the limpet and the lamprey both being noted for their suction capacity.

limpet

A limpet is a marine gastropod mollusk that clings tightly to rocks. A person who clings to someone or something can be called a *limpet*. And an explosive designed to cling to the hull of a ship is known as a *limpet*.

Lion

The English word *lion* for a type of large cat goes back to Greek *leon* ("lion"), which is perhaps of Semitic origin (compare Hebrew *labhi*, "lion").

beard, beard the lion in his den, take by the beard

In 1 Samuel 17:34-35 is the following passage: " ... and there came a lion ... and took a lamb out of the flock: And I went out after him and smote him, and delivered it out of his mouth: and when he arose against me, I caught him by his beard, and smote him, and slew him." From that passage come the modern expressions *to beard* meaning to confront boldly and *to take by the beard* meaning to attack resolutely. *To beard the lion in his den* has the added feature of saying that the "bearding" is done on the lion's (opponent's) own home ground.

better to be a live dog than a dead lion

(See *better to be a live dog than a dead lion* under "Dog.")

lion

The lion, a symbol of power, is known as "the king of the jungle." A man is sometimes called a *lion* in either a positive or a negative sense. In the positive sense, a *lion* is strong and courageous, as in "(as) brave (or bold) as a *lion*." That sense is influenced by such biblical passages as the following (Revelation 5:5): "And one of the elders saith unto me, Weep not: behold, the Lion of the tribe of Juda." In the negative sense, a *lion* is cruel and ferocious, as in "(as) savage as a *lion*." That sense, too, is influenced by biblical passages, such as the following (1 Peter 5:8): "Be sober, be vigilant; because your adversary the devil, as a roaring lion, walketh about, seeking whom he may devour."

About the year 1600, lions were kept in the Tower of London. They became a popular tourist attraction. People used to say that they had gone "to see the lions." Soon the word *lions* was used to refer to all kinds of famous places that people visited. Later the expression shifted from places to people, so that today any famous person can be called a *lion*.

lionhearted

To have the courage of a lion is to be *lionhearted*.

lion in the path

A dangerous obstacle, especially one invented as an excuse for inaction, is a *lion in the path* (or *way*). The origin of the phrase is in the Bible (Proverbs 26:13): "The slothful man saith, There is a lion in the way."

lionize

To treat a person as a celebrity is *to lionize* him (for *lion* meaning celebrity, see *lion* above).

lion's mouth

A place or situation of great danger is a *lion's mouth*. The origin of the expression is in such biblical passages as "Save me from the lion's mouth" (Psalms 22:21) and "I was delivered out of the mouth of the lion" (2 Timothy 4:17).

lion's share

The largest or best part of something is called the *lion's share*. The origin of this expression is in one of the fables ascribed to Aesop. The story comes in several different versions, but the essence of the tale is that a lion went hunting with some other animals (usually given as an ass, a fox, and a wolf) and together they killed a stag. When it came time to divide the meat, the lion claimed all of it and dared the others to challenge him. Originally, then, the *lion's share* was not merely the greatest part of something, but all of it.

twist the lion's tail

The British Lion is the national emblem of Great Britain. To insult or anger the people or the government of Great Britain is *to twist the lion's tail*.

Lizard

The English word *lizard* for a type of reptile goes back to Latin *lacertus* ("lizard"), which is related to *lacertus* ("muscle," originally the muscular part of the upper arm), which is based on an Indo-European root meaning "limb." The lizard, then, is named for its muscular appearance.

lounge lizard

The lizard has a reputation for remaining stationary for long periods of time. Thus, a foppish man who idles about the lounges of bars, cafés, and hotels with, or in search of, women is called a *lounge lizard*.

Loon

The English word *loon* for a type of bird is an alteration

(based on *loon*, "a worthless person") of earlier English *loom* ("loon"), which comes from Old Norse *lomr* ("loon"), which is based on an Indo-European root imitative of various sounds. The loon, then, is named for its cry.

crazy as a loon

The loon is noted for its clumsy gait on land, its wild actions in escaping from danger, and its gloomy cry. Therefore, an intensive for *crazy* is *(as) crazy as a loon*.

loon

A crazy person or a simpleton is a *loon*. This sense of the word *loon* probably combines a reference to the bird (see *crazy as a loon* above) and *loony*, which is actually a shortened alteration of *lunatic*.

Louse

The Modern English word *louse* for a type of insect goes back to Old English *lus* ("louse"), which is based on an Indo-European root meaning "louse."

louse

The louse is a small parasitic insect that sucks sap from plants or blood from animals. A detestable person is sometimes called a *louse*.

louse up

A louse can be said to damage its host, the plant or the animal. In fact, the mere presence of the louse creates an ugly atmosphere. Therefore, *to louse up* something is to spoil or ruin it.

lousy

Something filthy or mean or bad is thought to be, like the louse, *lousy*.

lousy with

Lousy also means full of lice. Therefore, to be full of, or well supplied with, anything at all is to be *lousy with* it.

Mackerel

The English word *mackerel* for a type of fish goes back to Old French *makerel* ("mackerel"), which is of uncertain origin.

dead as a mackerel

Many years ago, people used the expression *(as) mute as a fish* to mean silent. Being underwater, a fish is of course "silent" to humans. Later came *(as) mute as a mackerel* because the mackerel is a common fish and because the *m* of *mackerel* alliterates with the *m* of *mute*. Then, under the influence of *(as) dead as a herring* (see *dead as a herring* under "Herring"), the expression changed to *(as) dead as a mackerel*, meaning certainly dead.

holy mackerel

Since the earliest years of the Christian Era, Christians have symbolized Jesus by a fish. That practice is the probable origin of the colloquial expression of amazement *holy mackerel*, which is patterned after *Holy Ghost* and is of a type with *holy cow, holy Moses*, and so on. The expression was widely popularized by its frequent use on the *Amos and Andy* radio program beginning in the late 1920s. But it was already in use long before *Amos and Andy*, as seen in George Ade's 1899 *In Babel*: "Hot? Holy sufferin' mackerel!"

mackerel sky

The mackerel has wavy black stripes on its back. Small fleecy clouds that resemble the shape of those stripes can be called *mackerel clouds* or *mackerel-back clouds*. A sky spotted with such clouds is called a *mackerel sky*.

Magpie

The word *magpie* for a type of bird is a compound of two other English words: *Mag* (short for *Margaret*) and *pie* ("pie," the bird; see "Pie"). *Mag* is a common dialectal name for a chatterbox in English proverbial phrases. The magpie, then, is "the chattering pie (bird)."

magpie

Since the magpie is known for its noisy chatter, an incessantly talkative person is sometimes called a *magpie*.

Mammoth

The English word *mammoth* for an extinct type of elephant comes from obsolete Russian *mammot* ("mammoth"), which is based on Yakut *mamma* ("earth") or Tartar *mamont* ("earth") because the mammoth was believed to have burrowed.

mammoth

The mammoth was a huge prehistoric animal that looked much like the present-day elephant. Any enormous thing can now be said to have a *mammoth* size.

Mane

The Modern English word *mane* for a growth of animal hair goes back to Old English *manu* ("mane"), which is based on an Indo-European root meaning "neck."

mane

A mane is a growth of long hair on the back of the neck and shoulders of any one of various animals, especially the lion and the horse. Therefore, a growth of long hair on a person is sometimes referred to as a *mane*.

Mare

The Modern English word *mare* for a female horse goes back to Old English *mere* ("mare"), which is based on an Indo-European root meaning "horse."

mare's nest

A mare does not make a nest. Therefore, the proverbial expression *to find a mare's nest* means to find something supposedly wonderful but actually nonexistent. Today a hoax or a complicated situation is a *mare's nest*.

shanks' mare

The shank is the part of the leg between the knee and the ankle, or the whole leg itself. One's own legs are informally called *shanks' mare*, usually in the expression *to ride* (or *to go on*) *shanks' mare*, meaning to walk. The expression is based on a pun in which *shanks* is both the legs and a fictitious person named Shanks, who is mounted on a mare (of thin air).

Maverick

Samuel Augustus Maverick (1803-70) was a Texas pioneer and statesman. (His grandson Maury Maverick coined *gobbledygook;* see *to gobble* under "Animal Sounds" in Part Two.) He once let a herd of his unbranded cattle stray. His neighbors legally but unfairly caught and put their own brands on the cattle. Soon his neighbors, then everyone, began to refer to any unbranded or stray calf, cow, or steer on the range as a *maverick.*

maverick

A person who is extremely independent, especially one who refuses to conform to the opinions of his companions, is called (like an unbranded and freely roaming, and therefore "independent," calf) a *maverick.*

Mole

The Modern English word *mole* for a type of burrowing mammal is probably a shortening of *moldewarp,* a Middle English word for the same creature. *Moldewarp* is a combination of Middle English *molde* ("loose dirt") and *warp* ("to throw"). The mole, therefore, is "the dirt-thrower," referring to the animal's habit of kicking up dirt as it burrows. *Moldewarp* itself has a Germanic origin, the Modern German word for "mole" still being *Maulwurf.*

make a mountain out of a molehill

A molehill is a small mound of earth thrown up by a mole while it burrows its home. Anything small or insignificant can be called a *molehill.* To give great importance to something that is really unimportant is *to make a mountain out of a molehill*.

mole

A mole spends a great deal of its time underground and therefore in the dark. A person who works in the dark is sometimes called a *mole*.

Mongrel

The Modern English word *mongrel* for a dog of mixed breeds probably comes from Middle English *mong* ("mixture") with the diminutive suffix *-rel*. *Mong* itself comes from Old English *gemang* ("mixture"), which is related to *mengan* ("to mix") and is based on an Indo-European root meaning "to knead, fashion, fit."

mongrel

The word *mongrel* has been extended from its original dog-related sense, so that a person of mixed racial stock or a cross between one thing and another, especially if the result is inharmonious or indiscriminate, is a *mongrel*.

Monkey

The English word *monkey* for any one of various types of primates probably comes from, or is related to, Middle Low German *Moneke*, the name of the ape's son in the beast epic *Reynard the Fox*. *Moneke* in turn is based on any one of various old and modern Romance words that have the stem *mon-* for "ape" or "monkey" (Modern Spanish and Portuguese, for example, have *mono*). In English, the Romance *mon-* ("ape") is combined with the suffix *-key* ("little"). The monkey, then, is "the little ape."

The Romance *mon-* comes from the second syllable in the Turkish word *maymun* ("ape, monkey"), which comes from Arabic *maymun* ("ape, monkey"), a word that originally meant "lucky" and was applied euphemistically to the ape and the monkey, whose sight was believed to bring misfortune.

funny as a barrel of monkeys

To be hilarious is to be *(as) funny as a barrel* (or *barrelful*) *of monkeys*. However, the same expression is often used sarcastically to mean not funny at all.

make a monkey of

Monkeys have been forcibly made into entertainers and objects of ridicule by carnival people, organ grinders, and others. Therefore, to make a fool of someone is *to make a monkey of* (or *out of*) him.

monkey

A person who has some monkeylike characteristic (such as mischievousness or mimicry) is often called a *monkey*.

monkey around

To play casually is *to monkey around* (or *with*).

monkey business

Monkeys are noted for getting into mischief. Among humans, any improper conduct is said to be *monkey business*.

monkeyshine

A mischievous prank, such as a monkey (animal or human) might pull, is called a *monkeyshine* (often used in the plural).

monkey suit

Organ grinders used to dress their trained monkeys in short, tight jackets. A man's formal dress suit or uniform is sometimes called a *monkey suit* because it resembles the monkey's jacket.

monkey trick

Monkey trick (often used in the plural) is a synonym for *monkeyshine* (see *monkeyshine* above).

monkeywrench

A wrench having one fixed and one movable jaw at right angles to a straight handle is called, because of its appearance, a *monkeywrench*. Figuratively, something that disrupts is a *monkeywrench*.

Moose

The English word *moose* for a type of ruminant of the deer family is of Algonquian origin, recorded in different dialects as *mus*, *moos*, *moosu*, and others. The basic meaning of the word is "he trims or eats off smoothly," a reference to the fact that the animal strips and eats the bark from trees.

moose

A moose is a large mammal. A big man, a heavy woman, or any other large object can be called a *moose*.

Moth

The Modern English word *moth* for a type of insect goes back to Old English *moththe* ("moth"), which is based on an Indo-European root meaning "worm, gnawing vermin."

moth-eaten

In reference to the moth's characteristic of eating human clothing and leaving it in a tattered and useless state, any decayed condition can be described as being *moth-eaten*.

Mouse

The Modern English word *mouse* for a type of rodent goes back to Old English *mus* ("mouse"), which is based on an Indo-European root meaning "mouse."

burn the barn to get rid of the mice

To take extreme measures in solving a problem is, according to an old proverb, *to burn the barn* (or *house*) *to get rid of the mice* (or *rats*).

Mickey Mouse

The Walt Disney cartoon character Mickey Mouse has generated some figurative expressions. As an adjective,

Mickey Mouse means small, insignificant, petty. It also describes inferior dance-band music because such music is commonly played as background for cartoons. In film music, *Mickey-Mousing* (or *mickey-mousing* or *mickeymousing*) means presenting music in a simultaneous musical parody of the action on the screen (such as a descending scale as an object falls), a common procedure in cartoons.

mouse

The mouse is noted for its shyness; it dashes away and hides at the approach of any possible danger. Therefore, a timid person is sometimes referred to as a *mouse.*

A discolored lump caused by a blow near the eye is called a *mouse* because of the lump's resemblance to the shape and color of the rodent.

mousy

To be quiet, sneaky, or timid (like a mouse) is to be *mousy.*

play cat and mouse with

(See *play cat and mouse with* under "Cat.")

poor as a church mouse

A church is a bad place for a mouse to live: food is usually scarce. Therefore, among humans, to be extremely poor is to be *(as) poor as a church mouse.*

quiet as a mouse

Mice are noted for their quiet movement. Therefore, to be as noiseless as possible is to be *(as) quiet as a mouse.*

when the cat's away, the mice will play

(See *when the cat's away, the mice will play* under "Cat.")

Mule

The English word *mule* for the donkeylike animal goes back to Latin *mulus* ("mule").

stubborn as a mule

A mule, the offspring of a female horse and a male

donkey (jackass), is capable of doing much work. But when pushed too hard, the mule sometimes tries to save its strength, and its owner will call it stubborn and stupid for not moving fast enough. A person who is stubborn or stupid can be called a *mule*, commonly in the expression *(as) stubborn as a mule*.

white mule

Moonshine, a strong homemade liquor, is called *white mule* because of its lack of color and because of its powerful kick, figuratively like that of a mule.

Muzzle

The English word *muzzle* for the projecting jaws and nose of an animal goes back to Medieval Latin *musum* ("muzzle"), which is of uncertain origin.

muzzle

Since an animal's muzzle represents a potentially dangerous projection (because the animal might bite), the discharging end of a firearm is called the *muzzle*.

A *muzzle* is also a device fitted over an animal's snout to prevent the creature from eating or biting. Figuratively, something (such as censorship) that restrains free expression is a *muzzle*.

Nighthawk

The word *nighthawk* for a type of bird is formed quite simply from the words *night* and *hawk* ("hawk," the bird; see "Hawk"). This bird, however, is not really a hawk. It is a type of goatsucker and is related to the whippoorwill.

nighthawk

Soon after sunset, the nighthawk stirs into action and flies about all night feeding on insects. Among humans, anyone who often stays up or roams about late at night is a *nighthawk* (see *night owl* under "Owl" for a similar expression).

Nit

The Modern English word *nit* for the egg or the young of a louse or other parasitic insect goes back to Old English *hnitu* ("nit"), which is based on an Indo-European root meaning "egg of louse."

nitpick

Nits are characterized by their tininess. To search for and overemphasize small, trivial errors is *to nitpick.*

nitty-gritty

The *nitty-gritty* is the essential, accurate state of things. The expression was apparently first used by black Americans in the early 1960s. The reference may be to the gritlike nits that can get into the hair and scalp. Removing the unpleasant nits requires digging. And getting at the often unpleasant truth of a situation also requires digging.

Octopus

The English word *octopus* for a type of mollusk goes back to Greek *oktopous* ("eight-footed"), from *okto* ("eight") and *pous* ("foot").

octopus

Anything resembling the octopus, such as a person or an organization having many areas (or "arms") of influence or control, can be called an *octopus.*

Opossum

The English word *opossum* for a type of marsupial comes from a similar-sounding Algonquian name for the animal. The Indian name means "white animal."

The word *opossum* (pronounced *uh-PAHS-uhm*) is often shortened to *possum* (*PAHS-uhm)* in everyday speech.

play possum

When in danger, the opossum will lie motionless and pretend to be dead. Among humans, to pretend anything, especially illness or injury, is *to play possum.*

Owl

The Modern English word *owl* for a type of bird goes back to Old English *ule* ("owl"), which is based on an Indo-European imitative root meaning "to howl." The owl, then, is named for its cry.

night owl

Most owls hunt at night. Therefore, anyone who often stays up or roams about late at night is sometimes called a *night owl* (see *nighthawk* under "Nighthawk" for a similar expression).

solemn as an owl, wise as an owl

Athene was the patron goddess of ancient Athens. Since owls were abundant in the city, the owl became Athene's emblem. But Athene was also the Greek goddess of wisdom. Therefore, the owl became associated with wisdom.

The owl's appearance reinforces that association. Unlike most birds, the owl has a large, broad head with big, forward-pointing eyes (like human eyes). But the eyes cannot move in their sockets; the owl must move its entire head to see moving objects. Long lashes over the upper eyelids bob up and down with the opening and closing of the eyes. Popular belief has long associated the owl's broad head and blinking eyelashes with solemnity and wisdom. The truth, however, is that the owl is a relatively stupid bird. Geese, crows, and ravens are all smarter.

Nevertheless, a person thought to be solemn or wise is often compared to an owl, as in the familiar *(as) solemn as an owl* and *(as) wise as an owl.*

Ox

The Modern English word *ox* for a bovine mammal goes back to Old English *oxa* ("ox"), which is based on an Indo-European root meaning "to sprinkle." The ox, then, is originally "the besprinkler," that is, a male animal that can fertilize, or "sprinkle," a female. Today, however, *ox* usually refers to a castrated male, while *bull* refers to a fertile male.

ox

People have long referred to the ox as being big, strong, clumsy, and stupid. Any or all of those qualities may be intended when a person is called an *ox*.

Oyster

The English word *oyster* for a type of mollusk goes back to Greek *ostreon* ("oyster"), which is based on an Indo-European root meaning "bone." The oyster, then, is named for its hard, bonelike shell.

oyster

The oyster, like the clam, is commonly associated with the idea of being tightly shut; therefore, a closemouthed person, especially one who keeps a secret well, is sometimes called an *oyster*.

And because the oyster shell contains a desirable meat, anything from which one can extract something desirable can be called an *oyster*, as in "The world was his *oyster*."

Parrot

The English word *parrot* for a type of bird comes from dialectal French *perrot* ("parrot"), which may come from Old French *paroquet* ("parakeet") or from French *Perrot*, a pet variation of the personal name *Pierre* ("Peter").

parrot

Parrots can be taught to mimic human speech. The

birds, though, have no real understanding of what the words mean. A person who, without real understanding, merely repeats the words or imitates the actions of someone else can be called a *parrot*.

Paw

The English word *paw* for the foot of an animal goes back to Old French *poue* ("paw"), which probably comes from a Germanic form imitative of a pawing sound.

paw

The human hand is sometimes called a *paw*. To handle clumsily or with unwelcome familiarity (that is, in the manner of an animal) is *to paw*.

southpaw

A left-hander, especially an athlete, is a *southpaw*. The term originated as a baseball expression in the late 1800s because in most baseball parks home plate was situated to the west and the pitchers' mound to the east so that the setting sun would not be in the batters' eyes. A left-handed pitcher, then, would be pitching with his left hand, or *paw*, on the south side.

Peacock

The word *peacock* for a type of bird is a combination of two other English words: *pea* (from Latin *pavo*, "peafowl") and *cock* ("male fowl"). The peacock, then, is "the male peafowl."

peacock, proud as a peacock

The peacock is noted for its long, colorful tail feathers, which the bird can raise and spread into a beautiful fan. When the tail is raised, the peacock appears to be showing off. Among humans, a showoff is a *peacock*, and to be excessively proud is to be *(as) proud as a peacock*.

Pearl

The Modern English word *pearl* for a dense concretion of

abnormal growth within some mollusks comes from Middle English *perle* ("pearl"), which is adopted from Middle French *perle* ("pearl"), which goes back to Latin *perna* ("ham" or "sea mussel" attached to the ocean floor by a ham-shaped peduncle). The change from the *n* in Latin *perna* to the *l* of modern forms may be due to the influence of Vulgar Latin *pernula* (diminutive of *perna*) or of Latin *sphaerula* ("globule, little ball").

cast pearls before swine

Pearls are used as gems. To offer or give something of value to those unable to appreciate it is *to cast pearls before swine*. The source is in the Bible (Matthew 7:6): "Give not that which is holy unto the dogs, neither cast ye your pearls before swine."

pearl

One that is choice or precious is a *pearl*. Something resembling a pearl, such as a teardrop or a white tooth, is a *pearl*. *Pearl* is also a bluish gray color.

To form into small round grains is *to pearl*.

pearly

Pearly, besides meaning resembling pearls, means highly precious.

Pet

The origin of the word *pet* for a domesticated animal kept for pleasure rather than use is uncertain. But *pet* probably comes from Middle English *pety* ("small"), which comes from French *petit* ("small" or, as a noun, "little one").

pet

From the animal use of the word has come the idea of referring to a cherished or indulged person as a *pet*.

The noun has extended to a verb sense: to fondle or indulge is *to pet*.

Phoenix

The English word *phoenix* for a mythical bird goes back to

Latin *phoenix*, which is adapted from the Greek word for the bird, *phoinix*. The reason for the name is uncertain, but Greek *phoinix* also means "purple-red," the color of the bird's feathers, and "Phoenician," one from Phoenicia. The bird was held sacred in ancient Egypt, and the Greek word may have developed out of Egyptian *bynw, benu* ("phoenix").

phoenix

The phoenix, the only one of its kind, was said to live for five hundred years or longer in the Arabian Desert. Then it would burn itself, emerge from the ashes with renewed youth, and live another cycle. Today anything of excellence or beauty is sometimes called a *phoenix*. One that experiences a renewal after an apparent ruin is a *phoenix*.

Phoenix

When a certain place in Arizona was selected as the site of a new town in the 1860s, traces of an ancient Indian settlement were discovered there. Since a new city was expected to rise from the ashes (like the mythical bird), the city was called *Phoenix*.

Pie

The English word *pie* for a type of bird goes back to Latin *pica* ("magpie"), which is based on an Indo-European root meaning "woodpecker, magpie."

pie

The pie, more commonly known as the magpie, is noted for its black-and-white coloring. It is also noted for its habit of stealing miscellaneous little objects and storing them in a jumble. Either of those characteristics may be the reason for using the word *pie* to name a baked dish consisting of bits of meat, fruit, or other food enclosed in a crust. Reinforcing that possibility is the fact that the bird builds an extremely large nest—up to three feet in diameter—which is covered with a dome or canopy that clearly suggests the crust of the baked dish.

A parti-colored animal is a *pie*, short for *piebald* (see *piebald* below).

A mixed collection of printing type is a *pie*, or *pi*. The origin of this word is obscure, but this *pie* is probably ultimately related to the word for the bird.

piebald

The typical magpie is black with white markings. Therefore, to be two-colored, especially black and white, is to be *piebald* (*bald* here meaning marked with white). An animal, especially a horse, with such a coloring is a *piebald*. The adjective *piebald* also describes something composed of mixed or incongruous parts.

Pig

The Modern English word *pig* for a young swine comes from Middle English *pigge* ("pig"), which probably goes back to Old English unattested *picga* or *pigga* ("pig"), itself of uncertain origin.

buy a pig in a poke

(See *let the cat out of the bag* under "Cat.")

in a pig's eye

To make negative a previous affirmative statement, one can say *in a pig's eye*, meaning not at all, never, or nonsense. The origin of the expression is uncertain. But early quotations, in the late 1800s, refer to a popular shipboard game in which a person was blindfolded, turned around three times, and asked to locate the eye of a pig outlined on the deck. The odds against marking the correct place were great. Therefore, uttering something impossible is analogous to putting a mark *in a pig's eye*.

pig

The pig, a young hog, is commonly regarded as a dirty, gluttonous animal. Therefore, a dirty, gluttonous, or fat person can be called a *pig*. But the pig also has a more general reputation for leading a low, coarse way of life. Anyone who is disliked for almost any reason at all is sometimes called a *pig*.

piggyback

The word *piggyback*, meaning on the back or shoulders, has nothing to do with the animal. The word is an alteration of the earlier *pickaback*, of uncertain origin. Today, however, most people probably think of the pig when they say *piggyback*.

piggybank

For many years, a small pig-shaped bank for holding money, especially coins, has been called a *piggybank*. Today any small private bank, regardless of its shape, can be referred to as a *piggybank*.

pigheaded

The pig is generally thought to be stupid and stubborn. A person who displays stupidity or stubborness can be called *pigheaded*.

pig iron

Crude iron, because of its shape, is called *pig iron*.

pig Latin

Pig Latin is a playful code in speaking, a sort of mock Latin, presumably as pigs might speak it. Each word begins with its first vowel. Any preceding consonants are moved to the end of the word. And *-ay (ā)* is added to the result. *Pig Latin*, in pig Latin, is *igpay atinlay. Scram* is *amscray*.

pigpen/pigsty

Because of the pig's dirty pen, or sty, any dirty or untidy place can be called a *pigpen*, or *pigsty*.

pigtail

A tight, narrow braid of hair hanging down the back of the head is said to resemble the tail of a pig. Thus, the braid is called a *pigtail*.

Pigeon

The English word *pigeon* for a type of bird goes back to Old French *pijon* ("pigeon"), which comes from Late Latin *pipionem*, accusative of *pipio* ("young chirping bird, squab"), a derivative of the verb *pipire* ("to chirp"), which is based on an Indo-European imitative root meaning "to peep."

clay pigeon

In skeet and trapshooting, a clay target tossed into the air is called a *clay pigeon* because it substitutes for a real bird in practice shooting. A person who can easily be used by others for their own purposes is also called a *clay pigeon*.

pigeon

Pigeons are noted for being easily trapped. A person who is easily fooled can therefore be called a *pigeon*.

Pigeon is also a term of endearment for a girl or a woman.

pigeonhole

Pigeon lockers commonly have small holes (pigeonholes) in a wall or a door through which the birds can reach their nests. From that use of *pigeonhole*, the word has expanded in meaning to refer to any kind of small place for putting things, such as a drawer or a compartment in a desk or a cabinet. The use of the word has further broadened to include ideas as well as things, so that today to put ideas into definite places in an orderly system is *to pigeonhole* them.

pigeon-toed

Pigeon-toed means having the toes or the feet turned inward, like the feet of a pigeon.

stool pigeon

It was once common for a hunter to tie a pigeon to a stool to lure other pigeons. Therefore, a person who lures others into a trap or who informs on them (especially to the police) is called a *stool pigeon*.

Pinion

The English word *pinion* for the terminal section of a bird's wing (or, broadly, for the whole wing) goes back to Latin *pinna* ("feather, wing"), which is based on an Indo-European root meaning "to fly."

pinion

To pinion a bird is to cut off the pinion of one wing or to bind both wings so that the bird cannot fly. Among humans, then, to bind a person's arms or hands is *to pinion* him. The same idea can be expressed figuratively, as in "*to pinion* one to bad habits."

Pony

The English word *pony* for a small horse probably comes from obsolete French *poulenet* ("pony"), a diminutive of *poulain* ("foal"), which goes back to Latin *pullus* ("young animal"), which is based on an Indo-European root meaning "little."

pony

Something small for its kind is a *pony*. A literal translation of a text, especially one used surreptitiously by students, is a *pony*.

pony car

Any one of a certain group of two-door American hardtop autos is called a *pony car* because of its small size and lively performance.

ponytail

A hair style resembling the tail of a pony is called a *ponytail*.

Popinjay

The English word *popinjay* for the parrot goes back through French, Spanish, and Arabic forms to West African *pampakei* ("parrot"), a word of imitative origin. The English ending -*jay* is influenced by the bird name *jay*.

popinjay

Because of the popinjay's, or parrot's, gaudy plumage and mechanical repetition of words, a person given to vain displays and empty chatter is called a *popinjay*.

Pug

The origin of the word *pug* for a type of dog is obscure. Some authorities suggest that *pug* may be an alteration of *puck* ("mischievous sprite or elf"); others, that it may come from obsolete *pug*, a term of endearment for a person or a monkey.

pug nose

The pug has a snub nose. Hence, a human nose that is short, somewhat flattened, and turned up at the end is a *pug nose*.

Puppy

The English word *puppy* for a young dog goes back to Old French *poupee* ("doll"), which in turn goes back to Latin *pupa* ("girl, doll, puppet"), which is based on an Indo-European root imitative of a sucking sound and meaning "teat."

hush puppy

A ball of cornmeal dough fried in deep fat is a *hush puppy*, so called from the fact that it is sometimes used as food for dogs, who when satisfied will presumably become quiet. It is chiefly a Southern expression.

Hush puppy is also a trade name for a lightweight soft ("hush") shoe.

puppy

A puppy is any young dog, especially one less than a year old. Typically such a dog does not understand what its master expects in the way of proper behavior for a dog. A conceited or empty-headed young man is sometimes called a *puppy*.

puppy love

A temporary affection between a boy and a girl is called *puppy love*. (See also *calf love* under "Calf.")

Puss

The origin of the word *puss* for a cat is uncertain. But *puss* may originally be an attempt to imitate the spitting sound of the animal. Or it may be a survival of Old English *pusa* ("sack, bag," hence anything soft).

puss

Puss is sometimes used as a term of endearment for a girl or a woman.

pussyfoot

The cat is noted for its soft, cautious walking. A person who moves in such a manner can be said *to pussyfoot*. Extended, *to pussyfoot* means to act with caution or secrecy.

Quarry

The Modern English word *quarry* for a hunted animal comes from Middle English *querre, quirre* (originally "parts of a slain animal placed on its hide as the hound's reward," hence "a prey"), which derive from Old French *cuiree* ("quarry"), itself a blend of *cuir* ("hide, skin," from Latin *corium*, "hide, skin") and *coree* ("viscera," which goes back to Latin *cor*, "heart," which is based on an Indo-European root meaning "heart").

quarry

The original animal-related meaning of this word has extended, so that now any object of pursuit or attack can be called a *quarry*.

Rabbit

The origin of the word *rabbit* for a type of long-eared mammal is uncertain. But *rabbit* may go back to Old French *rabot* ("carpenter's plane"), in which case the rabbit would be "the animal resembling a plane." Or it may go back to Middle Dutch or Flemish *robbe* ("rabbit"), which in turn is probably a pet variation of the human name *Robert*.

jackrabbit start

Jackrabbit is short for *jackass-rabbit*, so called because the animal has long ears like the jackass. The jackrabbit is not really a rabbit. It is a hare, which is a larger animal than a rabbit. The jackrabbit is noted for its strong legs and quick start. Therefore, a fast, jerky start, especially by the driver of an automobile, is called a *jackrabbit start*.

pull a rabbit out of a hat

A familiar magic trick is to pull a rabbit out of a hat. Therefore, to do something by surprise or to give an answer when it seems impossible to do so is *to pull a rabbit out of a hat*.

rabbit

A coward or a timid person is a *rabbit*.

A figure of a rabbit sped mechanically along the route of a dog track for the dogs to chase is a *rabbit*. Similarly, a runner that sets a fast pace for the others in the first part of a long-distance race is a *rabbit*.

rabbit ears

Rabbit ears is the name of an indoor television antenna with two aerials that remind one of the ears of a rabbit.

rabbit punch

A short, sharp punch to the back of the neck is called a *rabbit punch*. There are at least two different versions of the origin of this term. One is that when a rabbit is annoyed by another rabbit, it will kick the offender in the back of the neck. The second version is that a gamekeeper will hit a rabbit in the back of the neck to put it out of pain. Today the expression *rabbit punch* is heard most often in boxing, where the punch is illegal.

Raccoon

The English word *raccoon* for a type of mammal comes

from a word in an Algonquian dialect of Virginia recorded in such forms as *rahaugcum, arocoun,* and *ärähkun.* The basic sense of the word is "he scratches with his hands," a reference to the raccoon's habit of leaving scratch marks on the bark of trees.

Coon is a familiar shortening of *raccoon.*

a coon's age

The raccoon does not hibernate; but during the cold months in the northern parts of the United States, the animal does sleep most of the time, waking only to feed and to mate. The animal thus disappears from human sight for long periods of time. Fancifully, then, a long time is *a coon's age.*

a gone coon

A person or a thing in a hopeless situation is, like the treed coon (see *tree the coon* below), *a gone coon.*

tree the coon

A raccoon is traditionally hunted by a pack of dogs. The chase usually ends when the raccoon is trapped in a tree. Therefore, to corner a person or to solve a problem is *to tree the coon.*

Ram

The Modern English word *ram* for a male sheep goes back to Old English *ramm* ("ram"), which is of Germanic origin and probably comes from, or is related to, another Germanic word meaning "strong."

battering ram

In ancient wars, a large beam of wood with iron at one end was used to beat down the walls of a besieged place. Since the running-and-bumping use of this engine suggested the behavior of a male sheep, the beam was called a *battering ram;* in fact, sometimes the iron end was in the form of a ram's head. Today any similar instrument, especially one used by firemen, is also called a *battering ram.*

ram

Because of the action of the animal, to strike or to cram or, figuratively, to force the passage or acceptance of is *to ram*.

Rat

The Modern English word *rat* for a type of rodent goes back to Old English *raet* ("rat"), which is of Germanic origin and may be based on an Indo-European root meaning "to scratch, gnaw," the animal being noted for its habit of chewing on or through things.

caught like a rat in a trap

To be trapped in a bad situation is to be *caught like a rat in a trap*.

drowned like a rat

Like (or *as wet as*) *a drowned rat* is an extremely old expression (going back at least to ancient Rome) that means soaking wet. Today, however, it is more common to find the expression *drowned like a rat*, meaning killed in a horrible way by drowning.

pack rat

The pack rat is a rodent noted for carrying away small objects and hiding them in its nest. A person who collects or hoards useless items is known as a *pack rat*.

rat

Rats have a bad reputation among humans because the rodents gnaw on household furniture, damage crops, carry disease germs, kill some domestic animals, and even attack helpless humans, especially newborn infants. Any hated person can be called a *rat*.

Rats are also said to abandon a house or a ship in trouble (see *desert a sinking ship* under "Animal-related Expressions" in Part Two). Therefore, anyone who deserts or informs on his fellows, especially during a time of trouble, can be called a *rat*. That idea is often expressed as a verb: to betray is *to rat*.

rathole

A hole used by, or the burrow of, a rat is known as a rathole. Any small and uncomfortable place, especially if dirty and disorganized, can be called a *rathole*.

rat race

Any fast-paced activity, especially a competitive one that leaves no time for relaxing or thinking, is called a *rat race*. *Rat* refers to the ugliness, and *race* to the speed, of the activity. The expression is a reference to laboratory rodents on a treadmill or in a race through the scientist's maze.

rats

Since rats have a general reputation for being disgusting animals, a common exclamation of anger or disgust is *rats*.

rattail comb

A hair comb having a narrow, pointed handle is called, because of its resemblance to the tail of a rat, a *rattail comb*.

rattrap

A rattrap is a device for catching rats. Among humans, any difficult or hopeless situation (as the rattrap is for the rat) is called a *rattrap*.

And since rats like to live in old, deserted structures, any dirty, run-down place can be referred to as a *rattrap*.

ratty

The adjective *ratty* literally means infested with, or suggestive of, rats. Because of the disgusting images created by the word, anyone or anything shabby or despicable is described as being *ratty*. *Ratty* also means angry, rats being noted for their fierceness.

smell a rat

Cats and dogs are able to smell a rat even when the rodent is hidden. Therefore, to suspect that something is wrong is *to smell a rat*.

Rook

The Modern English word *rook* for a bird related to the crow goes back to Old English *hroc* ("rook"), which is based on an Indo-European root imitative of a harsh voice and used as the base of various words representing loud noises or the names of birds.

rook

The rook is known for its cunning. It preys on other birds, steals farmers' seeds, and digs up young plants. Among humans, to cheat someone is *to rook* him. The cheater is a *rook*, as is the cheating itself.

rookie

A *rookie* is a recruit or a novice, especially a professional athlete in his first season. The word is probably an alteration of *recruit*, influenced by *rook* for the bird or a cheat or (obsolete) a dupe.

Rooster

The word *rooster* for an adult male bird or domestic fowl is built from the word *roost* and the suffix *-er*. The rooster, then, is "the one that roosts." (See also *roost* under "Animal Homes" and "Animal-related Expressions" in Part Two.)

rooster

Because of the characteristic behavior of an adult male domestic fowl, a cocky or vain person is called a *rooster*.

Rumen

The rumen is the first part of the stomach in a ruminating animal (ruminants include such animals as cattle, buffalo, deer, and camels). The English word *rumen* comes from Latin *rumen* ("throat").

ruminate

An animal that chews the cud (see *chew the cud* under "Cud") brings the cud up from an area of its stomach called the rumen, where food is stored and partially broken down. As Latin *rumen* ("throat") developed into English *rumen*, meaning the first stomach, so Latin *ruminare* ("to chew again") developed into English *to ruminate*, meaning to chew again or to chew the cud. At first, the English word *ruminate* was applied only to the animals that chewed the cud. But the idea of chewing again was later broadened to include thinking again. Therefore, among humans, to meditate or to go over and over again in the mind is *to ruminate* (meaning exactly the same thing as *to chew the cud*).

Rump

The Modern English word *rump* for the rear end of an animal comes from Middle English *rumpe* ("rump"), itself probably from Old Norse *rumpr* ("rump"), which is based on an Indo-European root meaning "to chop."

rump

Originally the word *rump* applied only to the hind part of the body of an animal. Later the sense extended, so that the rear end of a human being is now also referred to as a *rump*. In fact, the last or inferior part of anything can be called a *rump*.

Runt

The origin of the word *runt* for a small animal is uncertain. But *runt* is related to many Germanic words meaning "ox" or "cow," all of which go back to sources meaning "horned animal" and are ultimately based on an Indo-European root meaning "horn."

runt

A runt is an animal unusually small for its kind. A small person can be contemptuously called a *runt*.

Salamander

The English word *salamander* for a type of amphibian goes back through French and Latin words to Greek *salamandra* ("salamander").

salamander

The salamander is a lizardlike amphibian. In ancient folklore, the same name is applied to a mythical animal able to live in or endure fire without harm. Thus, any one of various fire-related objects—such as the residue iron at the bottom of a blast furnace, and certain types of stoves—is called a *salamander*.

Salmon

The English word *salmon* for a type of fish goes back to Latin *salmo* ("salmon"), which is related to *salire* ("to leap"), which is based on an Indo-European root meaning "to leap." The salmon, then, is "the leaping fish."

salmon

Because of the color of the fish, a light yellowish pink hue is called *salmon*.

Scale

The English word *scale* for one of the protective plates covering certain animals comes from Old French *escale* ("shell, husk"), which goes back to a Germanic word meaning "something split off," which in turn is based on an Indo-European root meaning "to cut."

scale

A small, thin, flat, rigid structure forming part of the external body of a fish, a reptile, or any one of various other animals is called a scale. That original sense of *scale* has extended. Some human diseases cause the skin to shed thin dry flakes of epidermis, each of which is called a *scale*. A coating that forms on heated metal (such as that of a kettle) is a *scale*. In general, a small, thin piece of anything is a *scale*.

Scallop

The English word *scallop* for a type of mollusk goes back to Old French *escalope* ("shell"), which goes back to a Germanic word meaning "something split off, scale, shell," which is based on an Indo-European root meaning "to cut, split."

scallop

The scallop is a type of bivalve mollusk characterized by a fan-shaped flat shell with a wavy outer edge. Anything that looks like a scallop—such as a thin slice of meat or one of a series of projections forming a border—can be called a *scallop*.

Sepia

The English word *sepia* for a cuttlefish goes back to Greek *sepia* ("cuttlefish"), which is related to *sepein* ("to rot, make putrid"). The sepia is named for its inky secretion.

sepia

Today the sepia is usually called the cuttlefish. The word *sepia* is applied to the cuttlefish's inky secretion or to a brown pigment from the ink. Hence, various shades of brown are called *sepia*, as is a print or a photograph of brown color.

Serpent

The English word *serpent* for a snake goes back to Latin *serpens* ("serpent"), which is also the present participle of Latin *serpere* ("to creep"), which is based on an Indo-European root meaning "to creep." Literally, then, the serpent is "the creeping thing."

serpent

Because of the reputation of the serpent, or snake, a

treacherous or malicious person is sometimes called a *serpent.*

serpentine

Anything resembling a serpent in form (such as a winding road) or in character (such as being wily or cunning) can be described as being *serpentine.*

Sheep

The Modern English word *sheep* for a type of mammal goes back to Old English *sceap* ("sheep"), which is of West Germanic origin but of uncertain meaning.

black sheep

A person who stands out from his group by being different or bad is called a *black sheep.* This expression may come from the idea that black wool is not so valuable as white, from the idea that black carries a traditional sense of evil, or perhaps from the idea that black sheep frighten the white ones.

lost sheep

In the Bible (Psalms 119:176) occurs this passage: "I have gone astray like a lost sheep." In religious contexts, the expression *lost sheep* has come to refer to someone who has strayed from the accepted teachings of his group. However, the expression has also broadened its meaning, so that any person who is thought to be on a course of self-destruction can be called a *lost sheep.*

separate the sheep from the goats

(See *separate the sheep from the goats* under "Goat.")

sheep

Sheep are noted for being timid and easily led. A person with similar qualities is also a *sheep.*

sheep's eyes

Shy lovesick glances are called *sheep's eyes* because of the gentle appearance of the eyes of sheep.

sheepskin

Diplomas used to be made of parchment from sheepskin. Today a diploma, regardless of the material, is often called a *sheepskin*.

shepherd

A shepherd is one who tends sheep. Figuratively, a pastor of a congregation, or "flock," is a *shepherd*. In biblical use, the word is applied to God, as in "The Lord is my shepherd; I shall not want" (Psalms 23:1); and to Jesus, as in "I am the good shepherd" (John 10:12).

wolf in sheep's clothing

(See *wolf in sheep's clothing* under "Wolf.")

Shell

The Modern English word *shell* for the hard covering of an animal goes back to Old English *sciell* ("shell"), which is based on a Germanic form meaning "a piece cut off, shell, scale," which is based on an Indo-European root meaning "to cut, split."

come out of one's shell

(See *crawl into one's shell* below.)

crawl into one's shell

When a snail or a turtle is disturbed, it will pull back into its shell. Among humans, to hide from any situation is *to crawl* (or *retreat*) *into one's shell*. To come back out and face the situation is *to come out of one's shell*.

Shitepoke

The word *shitepoke* consists of two parts: *shite* (an older spelling of the vulgar word for "excrement") and *poke* ("bag"). The bird is so named because of its habit of defecating when flushed.

shitepoke

Because of the shitepoke's traditional association with

excrement, the bird has a generally low reputation among humans. Hence, a rascal or a worthless person is called a *shitepoke.*

Shrew

The Modern English word *shrew* for a small mouselike animal goes back to Old English *screawa* ("shrew"), which is based on an Indo-European root meaning "to cut." The shrew is named for its pointed snout being a cutting tool.

shrew

It was at one time believed that the shrew is venomous or has a malignant influence. Therefore, a malicious person (originally anyone, but now a woman) with a violent temper and tongue is sometimes called a *shrew.*

Shrimp

The Modern English word *shrimp* for a type of crustacean comes from Middle English *shrimpe, schrimpe* ("shrimp"), which are related to *scrimman* ("to shrink"), which is based on an Indo-European root meaning "to bend, twist, shrink." The shrimp, then, is named for its shriveled appearance.

shrimp

Some large types of shrimp grow to a length of one foot. But the common shrimp is less than one inch long. A small or unimportant person is sometimes insultingly referred to as a *shrimp.*

Silk

The Modern English word *silk* for a type of fiber produced by silkworms goes back to Old English *sioloc, seoluc* ("silk"), which are of uncertain immediate origin but are related to Old Slavic, Latin, Greek, and other words that ultimately go back to Chinese *se, ssu* ("silk").

can't make a silk purse out of a sow's ear

(See *can't make a silk purse out of a sow's ear* under "Sow.")

silk, silken, silky

Thread or fabric made from the silkworm's fiber is *silk*. A garment made of this fabric is also *silk*, as in "She was dressed in *silk*." Any silklike material, such as the styles forming a tuft on an ear of corn, can be called *silk*. The plural, *silks*, refers to a distinctive silk uniform, as in "The jockey wore his *silks*."

Silken means resembling silk by being soft, smooth, delicate. The word is often used figuratively, as in *"silken flattery"* and *"silken* caress."

Silky is similar to *silken*, but *silky* also carries the senses of having silklike hairs and being seductive.

Skunk

The English word *skunk* for a type of mammal comes from the Algonquian language. The Indian word has been recorded in many different forms, such as *seganku, segonku,* and *squnck* (all meaning "skunk"). The original Indian sense seems to be "the mammal that urinates," a reference to the foul-smelling liquid that the skunk sprays.

drunk as a skunk

To be very drunk is to be *(as) drunk as a skunk*. The expression results from a simple rhyming pattern and correlates with the expression *stinking drunk*.

skunk

The skunk is known primarily for the noisome liquid it sprays when frightened. The odor of that liquid has given the skunk a reputation for being something to dislike and avoid. A mean or hated person is sometimes called a *skunk*.

To overwhelmingly defeat or to cheat someone (that is, to put a "stink" on him) is *to skunk* him.

Snail

The Modern English word *snail* for a type of mollusk goes back to Old English *snaeg(e)l* ("snail"), which is based on an Indo-European root meaning "to creep." The snail, then, is "the creeping thing."

snail

The snail is noted for being slow moving. A slow or lazy person can be called a *snail*.

snail's pace

An extremely slow rate of action is a *snail's pace*.

Snake

The Modern English word *snake* for a type of reptile goes back to Old English *snaca* ("snake"), which is based, like *snail*, on an Indo-European root meaning "to creep." The snake, then, is also "the creeping thing."

snake

A device for unclogging curved pipes is called, because of its appearance, a *snake*.

Snake is also short for *snake in the grass* (see *snake in the grass* below).

snakebitten

To be plagued by a series of problems is to be (like a person poisoned by a snake) *snakebitten* (or *snakebit*).

snake dance

A *snake dance* is an American Indian ceremonial dance in which snakes or snake images are handled.

Another kind of *snake dance* is a parade or a procession in which the players weave in a single file in a snakelike course.

snake eyes

A throw of two ones in dice is called, because of the two dots, *snake eyes*.

snake in the grass

According to an ancient Chinese proverb, "He who was bitten by a snake avoids tall grass." In the third chapter of

Genesis, Eve is betrayed by a serpent. The Roman poet Virgil, in his *Eclogues* (3.93), writes: *Latet anguis in herba* ("A snake lurks in the grass"). From these and other sources comes the idea of calling a hidden danger, especially from a secretly faithless friend, a *snake in the grass*.

snake oil

Any substance sold as medicine without regard for its true medical value is known as *snake oil*.

snake pit

A pit full of snakes creates an image of disorder and discomfort. Any place of chaos or tension can be called a *snake pit*; for example, a mental hospital marked by shabbiness and poor treatment of the patients is often referred to as a *snake pit*.

snaky

Snaky means suggestive of a snake. Figuratively, the word means treacherous or sly, as in *"snaky* insinuations."

Snipe

The English word *snipe* for a type of bird is related to *snip* and goes back to Old Norse *snipa* ("snipe"), which is related to many Germanic words meaning "beak." The snipe, then, is probably named for its long beak, with which the bird "snips" or "snaps."

guttersnipe

The snipe, which usually lives near marshes, feeds by poking its bill into the mud that lines a body of water. The bird is therefore associated with dirty habits. Since a gutter is one of the dirtiest places in a city, the bird developed the nickname of guttersnipe. Then a person who collected such things as rags and paper from street gutters began to be called a *guttersnipe*. Later a homeless child living in the streets was called a *guttersnipe*. Now the expression *guttersnipe* is applied to anyone who is thought to represent a low moral or economic position.

snipe

Because of the snipe's low reputation for living in swampy places, anyone who is thought to be a low-quality person can be called a *snipe* (or *guttersnipe*).

The snipe, living in soggy marshes and being a fast flier, is hard to shoot. Hunters have to set up at a distance, on solid ground, and take shots whenever they get a chance. That method of shooting snipes has also been applied to the attacking of humans: to shoot at a person from a concealed position or, figuratively, to aim harsh words at him is *to snipe* at him.

Snout

The Modern English word *snout* for the projecting nose and jaws of an animal comes from Middle English *snoute*, *snute* ("snout"), which probably derive from Middle Dutch *snute* ("snout"). The ultimate origin is an Indo-European root that represents a nasal sound and is used at the beginning of Germanic words connected with the nose—in the case of *snout*, perhaps specifically a root meaning "to drip fluid."

snoot, snooty

Snoot is a Scottish and American variant (based on Middle English *snute*) of *snout*. A human nose or face or grimace is a *snoot*. A snob is a *snoot*, and *snooty* means snobbish or exclusive, references to the upward tilt or thrust of the nose by a haughty person.

snout

The word *snout* was apparently first used in English for an elephant's trunk, then for the projecting nose and jaws of an animal. Something like an animal's snout, such as a nozzle, is also a *snout*. A human nose, especially a large one, is a *snout*.

Sow

The Modern English word *sow* for an adult female swine

comes from Middle English *sowe, suwe* ("sow"), which derive from Old English *sugu* ("sow"), which is based on an Indo-European root meaning "to produce" (the sow being noted for its prolific breeding) or on an Indo-European root imitative of the animal's sound.

can't make a silk purse out of a sow's ear

A silk purse is a delicate product. A sow's ear, on the other hand, is a coarse object. To say that one cannot make a high-quality product from poor material is to say that one *can't make a silk purse out of a sow's ear*.

Spawn

The English word *spawn* for the eggs of aquatic animals comes from the verb *to spawn* ("to produce or deposit eggs"), which goes back to Old French *espandre* ("to spread out"), itself from Latin *expandere* ("to spread out, expand"), which is based on an Indo-European root meaning "to spread." A spawn, then, is "that which is spread out" for hatching.

spawn

Since the mass of small eggs deposited by an aquatic animal is called a spawn, any offspring (especially a swarming brood) or the source (seed) of something can be called a *spawn*.

Among aquatic animals, to deposit eggs is to spawn. Therefore, to produce or generate anything is *to spawn* it.

Spider

The Modern English word *spider* for any one of various arachnids goes back to Old English *spithra* ("spider"), which is formed from *spinnan* ("to spin"), which is based on an Indo-European root meaning "to spin." The spider, then, is "the spinner" of webs.

spider

An evil person who lures others into traps (as the spider traps its victims in webs) can be called a *spider*.

spidery

Anything resembling a spider or a spiderweb, such as certain patterns of lace, can be described as being *spidery*.

Sponge

The English word *sponge* for a type of water animal comes from Latin and Greek *spongia* ("sponge").

sponge

The sponge is a water animal whose skeleton consists of soft, elastic fibers that can absorb large amounts of liquid. When the living matter is removed from a sponge, the remaining soft skeleton is used by humans for cleaning and bathing. A similar artificial object is also called a *sponge*. Any person or object that absorbs something (as a student might absorb his studies) is a *sponge*. A drunkard is a *sponge* who absorbs too much liquor. One who lives at the expense of others (that is, one who "soaks" up others' money) is a *sponge* (or *sponger*).

sponge cake

A cake with a light, spongelike texture is a *sponge cake*.

sponger

(See *sponge* above.)

throw in the sponge

In a boxing match, a sponge is used to clean off a fighter between rounds. A manager will sometimes literally throw the sponge into the ring as a signal to the referee that the manager and his fighter give up (a towel is often used for the same purpose). That idea has broadened, so that to give up in any kind of competition is *to throw in the sponge*.

Squirrel

The origin of the English word *squirrel* lies in the Greek word *skiouros* ("squirrel"), from *skia* ("shadow, shade") and *oura* ("tail"). The squirrel, then, is "the shadow-tail," that is, the animal that can cool off in the shade made by its own big, bushy tail.

squirrel away

Squirrels are known for their habit of storing food for the winter. Among humans, to hoard (anything) for future use is *to squirrel* (it) *away.*

squirrelly

Red squirrels are extremely noisy. They seem to be forever cutting and storing pine cones (up to one hundred per hour by each squirrel) and scolding one another all the while. From the behavior of the red squirrels has come the idea of describing an odd or crazy person as being *squirrelly.*

Stag

The Modern English word *stag* for an adult male deer comes from Middle English *stag, stagge* ("stag"), which go back to the probable Old English form *stagga* ("stag"), which is based on an Indo-European root meaning "to pierce, stick, sting." A stag, then, is originally "an animal provided with a male organ" with which a male "pierces" a female.

stag

As an adult male deer is known as a stag, so any man, especially one unaccompanied by a woman at a social gathering, can be called a *stag.*

stag party

A social gathering for men only, especially a party given for a bachelor just before his marriage, is a *stag party.*

Stork

The Modern English word *stork* for a type of bird goes back to Old English *storc* ("stork"), which is based on an Indo-European root meaning "stiff." The stork, then, is named for its stiff-legged walk.

stork, the stork is coming

In the ancient Greek mysteries, the stork goddess represents the archetypal woman, the bringer of life. In German and Dutch folklore, the belief is that storks pick up infants from marshes, ponds, and springs, where the souls of unborn children dwell; that idea is based on the worldwide belief that children are born first of the earth, their true mother. The storks then deliver the babies to humans. From the German and Dutch folklore comes an English expression meaning someone is pregnant: *the stork is coming*.

In American slang, *stork* means the process of giving birth. *To stork* is to give birth.

Stud

The Modern English word *stud* for a male horse kept for breeding purposes goes back to Old English *stod* ("stable for breeding horses"), which is based on an Indo-European root meaning "to stand," with the derived sense "place or thing standing."

stud

Stud originally denotes a stable where horses are kept for breeding, or the group of horses themselves. Only later, and originally only in the United States, did *stud* (short for *studhorse*) come to be applied to a single stallion. A human male is sometimes called a *stud* to emphasize his virility.

stud poker

Stud poker is poker in which some of the players' cards are dealt faceup, exposed to the other players (in a fearless, masculine—hence studlike—way.)

Swan

The Modern English word *swan* for a type of aquatic bird comes from Old English *swan* ("swan"), which is based on an Indo-European root meaning "to sound," which is applied to the swan because of the former belief that swans sing just before they die.

swan

The swan is noted for its white feathers, beautifully long neck, and graceful swimming. A person of unusual purity, beauty, or grace can be called a *swan*.

Because swans were at one time thought to sing just before they die (see *swan song* below), a singer or a poet has come to be referred to as a *swan*.

swan dive

Swans gracefully dip their long, curving necks far into the water to look for food. From the graceful appearance of the swan dipping into the water has come the name of a human dive: the *swan dive*. The *swan dive* is a forward dive performed with the head back, the back arched, and the arms spread sideways in midair and then brought together above the head as the diver enters the water. (In England, this dive is sometimes called a *swallow dive*.)

swan song

Swans do not sing. They honk. Some honk with loud, resonant voices. Others with softer voices. The "mute" swan hisses and grunts only, and in flight it produces a sighing whistle by its wings on the downstroke. In ancient Greece, Apollo, the god of music, was associated with the swan because of the belief that the swan, after a lifetime of not singing, is suddenly able to sing just before it dies. From that belief has come the custom of referring to the final work of any artist, group, or period as a *swan song*.

Swine

The Modern English word *swine* for a hog goes back to Old English *swin* ("swine"), which is based on an Indo-European root imitating the animal's sound and meaning "pig, sow."

cast pearls before swine

(See *cast pearls before swine* under "Pearl.")

swine

The word *swine*, like *hog*, brings to the popular mind an

animal noted for its coarse and dirty living habits. A coarse, dirty, or hated person is sometimes referred to as a *swine*.

Tadpole

The Modern English word *tadpole* for the aquatic, immature form of such animals as frogs and toads comes from Middle English *taddepol*, which is compounded from *tadde* ("toad") and *pol* ("head"). The tadpole, then, is literally "the toad head."

tad, tadpole

A small child, especially a boy, is sometimes affectionately called *tadpole* or simply *tad*.

Tail

The Modern English word *tail* for the rear end, or a prolongation of the rear end, of the body of an animal goes back to Old English *taegel* ("tail"), which is based on an Indo-European root meaning "fringe, lock of hair, horsetail." A tail, then, is originally "a hairy appendage"; the word has come, of course, to refer to any kind of tail, with or without hair.

bobtail

One meaning of the verb *to bob* is to cut short. An animal (especially a horse or a dog) with its tail cut short has long been called a bobtail. Figuratively, anything cut short or abbreviated can be called a *bobtail*.

curtail

In the sixteenth century, English borrowed the French word *courtault* (from *court*, "short," and the suffix *-ault*), which had various meanings, including "a short, dumpy man," "a short piece of artillery," and "a horse or a dog with a docked tail." The animal meaning was the usual one in English. English writers quickly shortened the word to *curtal* and then began to confuse the second syllable with the English word *tail*. Therefore, while the word *curtal* was extending its sense to become a verb meaning to shorten or abridge anything in any manner, the spelling was changing to the modern *to curtail*.

have a tiger by the tail

(See *have a tiger by the tail* under "Tiger.")

make head or tail of

A coin has a "heads" side and a *tails* side (see *tails* below). A coin is often flipped so that a decision can be made according to which side lands facing up. Figuratively, to make sense of anything is *to make head(s) or tail(s) of* it.

put salt on its tail

Children are often told that they can catch a bird by putting salt on its tail. That advice is often referred to in extended senses, so that to catch or to somehow hamper someone or something is *to put* (or *lay* or *throw*) *salt on its* (or *one's*) *tail*.

ragtag and bobtail

As mentioned (see *bobtail* above), a bobtail is an animal with its tail cut short. Formerly, a disliked person was also called a *bobtail*. Gradually the word has become part of a longer expression that refers to a whole group of people as being riffraff or rabble: the *ragtag and bobtail*.

tail

The word *tail* can be applied to anything that resembles an animal tail, such as the *tail* of a kite, the *tail* of a comet, or the *tail* of a music note. More broadly, anything having to do with the back or the bottom or the last part of something can be called a *tail* or a *tail end*.

To connect end to end or to follow close behind is *to tail*. To disappear gradually or to merge into is *to tail (off)*, as in "The ships *tail off* over the horizon."

tail along

To follow without participating is *to tail along*.

tailback

In football, the offensive back who lines up farthest behind the line of scrimmage is known as the *tailback*.

tailcoat

A man's dress coat with a pair of tapering skirts, or *tails*, at the back is called a *tailcoat*.

tailgate

At the rear of a vehicle, a board or a gate that can be removed or let down is called a *tailgate*. From that object has come the idea that to drive dangerously close behind another vehicle is *to tailgate*.

taillight

A *taillight* is a warning light, usually red, at the rear of a vehicle.

tailpiece

A piece added at the end, such as a certain part on a violin or an ornament at the end of a printed text, is a *tailpiece*.

tailpipe

A pipe discharging exhaust gases rearward is a *tailpipe*.

tails

On a coin, the reverse of the "heads" (portrait) side is the *tails* side.

Tails is also short for *tailcoat* (see *tailcoat* above).

tailspin

The downward spiral of an aircraft is a *tailspin*. Figuratively, a mental or emotional collapse is a *tailspin*.

tail wagging the dog

(See *tail wagging the dog* under "Dog.")

tail wind

A wind coming from directly behind an airplane or a ship is called a *tail wind*.

turn tail

To turn one's back and run away is *to turn tail*, as an animal literally turns its tail to escape.

twist the lion's tail

(See *twist the lion's tail* under "Lion.")

two shakes of a lamb's tail

(See *two shakes of a lamb's tail* under "Lamb.")

with one's tail between one's legs

A dog characteristically drops its tail between its legs when it is frightened or beaten. Among humans, to be humiliated or defeated is to be *with one's tail between one's legs*.

Tiger

The English word *tiger* for a large member of the cat family goes back to Latin and Greek *tigris* ("tiger"), which is adapted from an Iranian word related to Avestan *tigri* ("arrow") and *tigra* ("sharp, pointed"), which are based on an Indo-European root meaning "to stick, pierce; sharp, pointed." The tiger, then, is literally "the animal whose spring is arrow swift."

have a tiger by the tail

To find oneself in a situation more difficult to handle than one expected is *to have a tiger by the tail*. The expression is a natural metaphor, though it may have evolved from a specific folktale, such as "Little Black Sambo," or from a specific earlier expression, such as the Chinese proverb "He who rides a tiger is afraid to dismount."

paper tiger

One who, or that which, seems powerful but is really weak or ineffective is a *paper tiger*. The expression came to prominence in 1946 when it was applied to the United States by Communist China's Mao Tse-tung, who probably derived it from a Chinese proverb.

tiger, tigress

A person resembling a tiger in fierceness or courage can be called a *tiger* (male) or a *tigress* (female).

A *tiger* is also a loud yell, sometimes the word *tiger* itself, following a round of enthusiastic cheering, as in "three cheers and a *tiger*." This use of the word originated in the 1820s in the United States. According to an early quotation, soldiers of the Boston Light Infantry were called *tigers* because of their rough behavior at a public event. The soldiers, who were proud of the name, later incorporated a tigerlike growl at the end of some public maneuvers. Hence, a yell at the end of vocal maneuvers (cheers) is a *tiger*.

tigereye

A type of yellowish to grayish brown ornamental stone is called a *tigereye*.

tigerish

To be fiercely cruel, aggressive, or bloodthirsty is to be *tigerish*.

Toad

The Modern English word *toad* for a type of amphibian goes back to Old English *tade, tadige* ("toad"). Earlier connections with other languages are uncertain.

toad

The toad is similar to the frog. But the toad has shorter legs and is generally clumsier. The toad usually has warts on its skin and a poisonous liquid in the bumps just behind its eyes. Because of the toad's rather disgusting appearance, a contemptible person or thing is sometimes called a *toad*.

toadstool

A certain fungus having an umbrellalike cap is called a *toadstool* (usually inedible as opposed to the edible mushroom). It is a fanciful name implying that the plant might make a good stool for a toad to sit on.

toady

Phony medicine men used to perform public shows to attract customers. The medicine man would let his assistant eat or pretend to eat a toad, which was widely believed at the time to be poisonous. Then the master would "cure" the assistant with a tonic and sell the "medicine" to the audience. The assistant was soon known as a *toadeater*. Later to be a *toadeater* or *to eat (anyone's) toads* meant to please someone else by doing or being something revolting. Today the expression has been shortened to *toady*, a fawning flatterer.

ugly as a toad

To be very ugly is to be *(as) ugly as a toad* (see *toad* above).

Tortoise

The Modern English word *tortoise* for a type of reptile comes from Middle English *tortuce* ("tortoise"), which comes from Late Latin *tortuca* ("tortoise"). The ultimate origin is uncertain. But some authorities speculate that *tortuca* is a variant (influenced by Latin *tortus*, "twisted," in reference to the reptile's crooked feet) of Vulgar Latin *tartaruca* (based on an earlier Greek word), meaning "tortoise" or "beast of Tartarus" (Tartarus, in classical mythology, being a place in Hades for the punishment of the wicked). The ancients called the tortoise the "beast of Tartarus" because it has "twisted" feet, as wicked people have "twisted" minds or hearts.

tortoise

The tortoise, like the closely related turtle, is noted for its slow movement. Any slow-moving person or thing can be called, or compared to, a *tortoise*.

Tripe

The English word *tripe* for animal stomach tissue is adopted from Old French *tripe* ("tripe"), which perhaps comes ultimately from Arabic *tharb, therb* ("entrails, fold of fat" or "net, fold of cloth").

tripe

Tripe is the stomach tissue of a ruminant—especially an ox, a sheep, or a goat—used as food. Anything worthless, offensive, or false can be called *tripe*.

Turkey

The word *turkey* was at one time applied to the guinea fowl, a West African bird imported to Europe via the Middle Eastern country of Turkey. Later a large American bird was discovered that people, by confusion with the guinea fowl, began to call a turkey. Soon the word *turkey* was dropped for the guinea fowl and kept for the American bird.

cold turkey

Cold turkey has three basic and related meanings: blunt language or procedure; a cold, aloof person; and a sudden halt to the use of a drug by an addict. There are also adjective *(cold-turkey)* and adverb *(cold turkey)* parallels. More broadly, *cold turkey* means without preparation, as in "He did the job *cold turkey*."

The reason for the expression is uncertain. But *cold* and *turkey* have histories that logically lead to their being welded together. *Cold* has meant without warmth, then (since the 1100s) without intensity of feeling, then (since the late 1800s in America) absolutely or without mitigation, as in "She turned him down cold." *Turkey* has been used since the mid-1800s in the phrase *to talk* (or *say*) *turkey* (see *talk turkey* below) to mean bluntness or facts. By the early 1900s, the words *cold* (without mitigation) and *turkey* (facts) were joined in the phrase *to talk cold turkey*, meaning to speak the plain truth. Later *cold turkey* (plain truth) was used alone to mean blunt language, an aloof person, or a sudden halt to drug use. All of these senses are probably reinforced by the stark image of a dead turkey that is plucked and uncooked.

talk turkey, say turkey to (one) and buzzard to (another)

By the mid-1800s in the United States, *to talk* (or *say*) *turkey* meant to speak pleasantly or plainly. In a well-known anecdote of the period, a white man and an Indian went hunting together and killed a turkey and a crow (in some versions, a buzzard). The white man, trying to cheat the Indian, said, "You may have your choice. You take the crow and I'll take the turkey, or if you'd rather, I'll take the turkey and you take the crow." The Indian replied, "You no talk turkey to me a bit" or "You never once said turkey to me." A common later expression was *to say turkey to (one) and buzzard to (another)*, meaning to give (one) the advantage over (another).

Turkey may have been selected for this expression simply because the bird was such an important food in frontier America. To talk about turkey was to talk about something pleasant or serious (requiring plain talk). But there were also a couple of American folk influences leading to the use of the word *turkey*. One was that white men constantly wanted to talk turkey with Indians (that is, to talk plainly about trading white men's goods for the Indians' delicious turkeys). Another influence was an old frontier joke about turkeys filling the air with their loud love calls. All a hunter had to do was to imitate the turkey call, and the turkey would come right out in the open as an easy target. Both the turkey and the hunter, then, showed no modesty in their open love calls; they spoke bluntly when they "talked" turkey.

turkey

The turkey is noted for being rather ugly and awkward—a "loser" in appearance. A person, object, or event (such as a theatrical production) without appeal or success can be called a *turkey*.

Turtle

The English word *turtle* for a type of reptile is probably an adaptation, originally by English sailors, of French *tortue* ("tortoise"). The English sailors were influenced by the fact that they were already familiar with the word *turtle* for an animal, specifically a bird (see "Turtledove").

turn turtle

Long ago, on Caribbean islands, English sailors saw that a native could capture a large, heavy sea turtle by grabbing one of the reptile's flippers and turning the turtle on its back, rendering it helpless. Later the sailors noticed that a capsized ship reminded them of a turtle turned on its back; therefore, it was said of any vessel that to capsize or overturn was *to turn the turtle*. Today the shortened form of *to turn turtle* means to turn upside down, and it can refer to any object.

turtle

The turtle, like the closely related tortoise, is noted for its slow movement. Any slow-moving person or thing can be called, or compared to, a *turtle*. (It should be mentioned, however, that not all turtles are slow. Sea turtles swim quite fast. And on land, one species in North America can actually outrun a man on level ground.)

turtleneck

A high, close-fitting collar is called, because it resembles the shell around the neck of a turtle, a *turtleneck*. The word is most commonly found as an adjective, as in *"turtleneck* sweater."

Turtledove

The Modern English word *turtledove* for a type of bird goes back to Old English *turtle* ("turtledove"), itself from Latin *turtur* ("turtledove"), which represents an attempt to imitate the cooing of the bird.

turtledove

The turtledove is noted for its shyness, sad cooing, and affection for its mate. Among humans, a sweetheart is sometimes called a *turtledove*.

Urchin

Urchin is an archaic English word for the hedgehog. *Urchin* can be traced back to Middle English *irchoun* ("hedgehog"), which goes back through Old French *hericun* ("hedgehog") to Latin *er* ("hedgehog") to an Indo-European root meaning "to bristle, be stiff," a root applied to the hedgehog in reference to the animal's spines.

urchin

A hedgehog (formerly called an urchin) may be said to be an irritating animal because of the danger of being stuck by its spines. Hence, a mischievous youngster is an *urchin*.

Vermin

The English word *vermin* for any small revolting animal goes back to Latin *vermis* ("worm"), which is based on an Indo-European root meaning "to bend, turn, twist." Vermin, then, are named for the worm's squirming motion.

vermin

Small common animals (such as flies, lice, bedbugs, and rats) that are thought to be harmful or disgusting are called vermin. An obnoxious person is sometimes referred to as a *vermin.*

Viper

The English word *viper* for any one of several types of poisonous snakes goes back to Latin *vipera* ("viper"). *Vipera* is formed from two other Latin words: *vivus* ("living") and *parere* ("to bring forth"). This combination of Latin words is applied to the viper in reference to the fact that true vipers bring forth living young rather than eggs.

nourish a viper in one's bosom

There is an ancient fable about a frozen viper (or snake). A farmer, taking pity on the viper, picked up the reptile and warmed it by placing it on his bosom. Later, after the viper thawed out, it bit (or tried to bite) the farmer (or, in another version, one of the farmer's children). Therefore, to help someone who turns out to be ungrateful and treacherous is *to nourish a viper in one's bosom.*

viper

Any evil or spiteful person (that is, one with a "poisonous" attitude) can be called a *viper.* A *viper* is also a disloyal person (see *nourish a viper in one's bosom* above).

Vixen

The Modern English word *vixen* for a female fox comes from a dialect in southern England. That *vixen* comes from Middle English *fixen* ("she-fox"), which goes back to Old English *fyxe* ("she-fox") or to Old English *fyxen* (originally "of a fox," then "she-fox"), both of which are based on the same Indo-European root as *fox* (see "Fox").

vixen

An ill-tempered woman is sometimes called a *vixen.*

Vulture

The English word *vulture* for a type of bird goes back to Latin *vultur* ("vulture"), which is related to *vellere* ("to tear"), which is based on an Indo-European root meaning "to tear." The vulture is named "the tearing bird" for the way that it tears meat from carcasses.

vulture

The vulture is an ugly bird with dark feathers and a naked head. It feeds primarily on carrion. One who exploits or preys on others (especially those in distress) can be called a *vulture.*

Walrus

The English word *walrus* for a type of marine mammal is adopted from the same word in Dutch, which comes from a Scandinavian source akin to Danish *hvalros* ("walrus"), which goes back to Old Norse *hrosshvalr*, a compound of *hross* ("horse") and *hvalr* ("whale"). Old Norse *hvalr* is based on an Indo-European root meaning "big fish." The walrus, then, is originally "the horse whale" or, in its modern form, "the whale horse."

walrus mustache

A thick shaggy mustache hanging down loosely at both ends (like the one on a walrus) is called a *walrus mustache*.

Wasp

The Modern English word *wasp* for a type of insect goes back to Old English *waesp* ("wasp"), which is based on an Indo-European root meaning "to weave." The wasp, then, is "the weaver" of a weblike nest.

waspish

Anyone or anything resembling a wasp in behavior (such as being snappish or petulant) or in form (such as being slightly built) can be described as being *waspish*.

Wax

The Modern English word *wax* for a substance produced by bees goes back to Old English *weax* ("beeswax"), which is based on an Indo-European root meaning "wax," which is related to another root meaning "to weave." Wax, then, is named for its appearance of having been "woven" by the bees.

wax

Any natural or artificial substance resembling beeswax (such as that used in candles, paper coatings, or polishing materials) is called *wax*. Anything likened to wax as being soft and readily molded is also *wax*.

waxy

To resemble wax by being pale, smooth and lustrous, or pliable is to be *waxy*.

Weasel

The Modern English word *weasel* for a type of mammal goes back to Old English *wesule, wesle* ("weasel"), which are based on an Indo-European imitative root meaning "to break wind" or "to flow out." The weasel, then, is named for its characteristic stench: "the malodorous animal."

weasel

The weasel is known for being sneaky and able to squeeze through small holes. It often enters chicken coops and kills more chickens than it can eat. A sneaky, despised person can be referred to as a *weasel*.

weasel out

To equivocate (see *weasel word* below) or to escape from or evade a situation or obligation is *to weasel out*. The reference is to the way a weasel avoids trouble by squirming through small holes.

weasel word

It is said that the weasel can suck the contents out of an egg while leaving the shell apparently intact. Therefore, a word of an equivocal nature used to deprive a statement of force or to evade or retreat from a direct statement is called a *weasel word* because the word is like the egg—empty. Theodore Roosevelt once gave an example: "You can have universal training, or you can have voluntary training, but when you use the word *voluntary* to qualify the word *universal*, you are using a weasel word; it has sucked all the meaning out of *universal*. The two words flatly contradict one another."

Wether

The Modern English word *wether* for a castrated ram goes back to Old English *wether* ("wether"), which is based on an Indo-European root meaning "year." A wether, then, is originally "a yearling" or "a one-year-old male sheep."

bellwether

A bellwether is a wether that leads the flock of sheep and usually wears a bell. Therefore, any person, group, place, or thing that takes the lead or initiative in any kind of activity can be called a *bellwether*.

Whale

The Modern English word *whale* for a type of sea mammal goes back to Old English *hwael* ("whale"), which is based on an Indo-European root meaning "big fish."

whale

The whale is a huge sea mammal. Therefore, something extremely big or impressive in any way can be called a *whale*.

(*To whale* meaning to beat may come from the former practice of beating with a whalebone whip, but the origin of this use of the verb *to whale* is uncertain.)

Whelp

The Modern English word *whelp* for the young of various animals (especially the dog) goes back to Old English *whelp* ("whelp"), which is based on an Indo-European root meaning "to yelp, cry out."

whelp

When the word *whelp* is applied to a young human, the term is generally meant as an insult. By extension, any despised person, even an adult, can be contemptuously referred to as a *whelp*.

Wildcat

The word *wildcat* for a member of the cat family is a simple combination of *wild* and *cat* (see "Cat").

wildcat

The wildcat, larger and stronger than a domestic cat, is known for its viciousness. A quick-tempered, savage person can be called a *wildcat*.

Any project involving risks or recklessness can be referred to as a *wildcat*, such as an exploratory oil well, a poorly planned business, or an unsanctioned labor strike.

Wing

The Modern English word *wing* for a type of animal appendage goes back to Middle English *wenge* ("wing"), itself from Old Norse *vaengr* ("wing"), which is based on an Indo-European root meaning "to blow," from which also comes the English word *wind*. A wing, then, is "that which flutters in the wind."

clip one's wings

A bird with clipped wings cannot fly. Therefore, to cripple one's ability to accomplish something is *to clip one's wings*.

earn one's wings

Upon passing rigid requirements, a pilot is awarded a wing-shaped badge, which is therefore a symbol of proficiency. To prove oneself able in any skill, then, is *to earn one's wings*.

in the wings

In its original sense, *in the wings* means to be out of sight in the *wings* (see *wing it* below) of a theater stage. Extended, *in the wings* means to be in the background but close at hand, as in "The second-string quarterback was waiting *in the wings*."

on the wing

To be active in any way is to be (like a flying bird) *on the wing*.

sprout wings

Angels are conventionally depicted as having wings. Therefore, to perform good deeds or to develop a divine nature is *to sprout wings*.

take wing

To leave in a hurry is (like a bird taking off) *to take wing*.

try one's wings

To attempt for the first time to do something on one's own is (like the young bird on its first flight) *to try one's wings*.

under one's wing

A bird protects its chicks by putting them under its wing. To put people or things in one's care is to put them *under one's wing*.

wing

A human arm can informally be referred to as a *wing*. A *wing* is also any inanimate object resembling a bird's wing, such as the *wing* of a plane or the *wing* of a building.

To fly, in an airplane or otherwise, is *to wing*. Figuratively, one's spirit or inspiration can also *wing*.

wingback

In football, an offensive back who lines up outside the tight end is called a *wingback*.

wing it

In a theater, a piece of scenery at the side of the stage is called a *wing* because it is an appendage to the stage. The *wings* are the backstage areas to the right and the left of the stage. *To wing it* means to act without having learned one's lines, relying on prompting from the wings or on quick glances at one's part in the wings before going onstage. The meaning of the phrase has extended, so that to improvise any activity is *to wing it*.

wing tip

A shoe style that brings to mind a wing is called a *wing tip*.

Wolf

The Modern English word *wolf* for a type of predatory mammal goes back to Old English *wulf* ("wolf"), which is based on an Indo-European root meaning "wolf" and may be related to a root meaning "to tear," making the wolf "the tearing animal."

cry wolf

In a fable, a shepherd boy made fun of his neighbors by repeatedly crying "Wolf!" and watching them scramble in fear. One day a wolf really came, but no one would believe the boy when he cried "Wolf!" Today to give a false alarm is *to cry wolf*.

keep the wolf from the door

To keep the wolf from the door means to avoid poverty or starvation. There are at least two possible origins for this old expression. One is related to the fact that the expression originated long ago when many households depended on their domestic animals for a livelihood. If a wolf came close to the house and killed the family's animals, the humans would be forced into poverty and starvation. Furthermore, if the humans starved to death, the wolf might come right up to the door to devour the deceased people themselves. Therefore, *to keep the wolf from the door* was to keep the wolf from eating the family's animals and from eating the family itself.

The other possible origin is simply that the wolf, because of its ravenous appetite, is a symbol of hunger. Therefore, *to keep the wolf from the door* is to keep hunger from the house.

lone wolf

Wolves usually live in packs of eight or more members. Sometimes, however, one leaves the pack and becomes a lone wolf. It travels alone until it finds a mate, has pups, and starts a new pack. A person who lives, acts, or works alone can be called a *lone wolf*.

sea wolf

The wolffish is a large, fierce, ravenous ocean fish. A pirate, because he reminds people of the fearsome wolffish and of the predatory land wolf, is sometimes called a *sea wolf*.

throw to the wolves

To ruthlessly sacrifice (another person) to protect oneself is *to throw* (the person) *to the wolves*.

wolf

The wolf is known for its fierce attack and its ravenous appetite. A cruel, destructive person can be called a *wolf*.

A man who seems to be "hungry" for many women and is direct when he amorously approaches ("attacks") them is often referred to as a *wolf*.

To gobble food down quickly (as a wolf does) is *to wolf* it down.

wolf call

A whistle, shout, or call of any kind made by a man admiring a woman is known as a *wolf call* (or *whistle*, if a whistle) because such a call is characteristic of the human *wolf* who is "hungry" for and "attacks" many women (see *wolf* above).

wolf in sheep's clothing

A *wolf in sheep's clothing* is a person who hides his harmful intentions under an innocent or friendly appearance. This expression has been popularized through two important ancient sources. One is the fable about a wolf that wrapped itself in a sheepskin to hide among the sheep and kill them. The other is in the Bible (Matthew 7:15): "Beware of false prophets, which come to you in sheep's clothing, but inwardly they are ravening wolves."

Wool

The Modern English word *wool* for the coat of a sheep goes back to Old English *wull* ("wool"), which is based on an Indo-European root meaning "wool," which is related to another root meaning "to tear, pull." Wool, then, is "that which is pulled or shorn off."

all wool and a yard wide

Literally, *all wool and a yard wide* refers to fabric and means of pure quality and of full measure. Figuratively, the expression refers to a person or a thing and means genuine, of superior quality.

dyed-in-the-wool

Dye is more deeply absorbed into wool before the wool is spun into yarn. Figuratively, to be thoroughgoing or uncompromising is to be *dyed-in-the-wool*, as in "a *dyed-in-the-wool* sports fan."

in one's wool

To be persistently annoying (that is, in one's "hair") is to be *in one's wool*.

pull the wool over one's eyes

To delude or deceive one is *to pull the wool over one's eyes*.

wild and woolly

In the late 1800s, the American Far West was described as being *wild and woolly* because parts of it were lawless and crude. According to an 1891 publication, "Woolly...seems to refer to the uncivilized—untamed—hair outside—wool still in the sheepskin coat—condition of the Western Pioneers." The sense of the expression has extended, so that now to be boisterous, untamed, or unrefined is to be *wild and woolly*.

wool

Anything resembling wool, such as the dense felted pubescence on a plant or the hairy coat on some insects, is called *wool*.

woolgathering

It was once common among the rural poor in England to wander about the countryside collecting tufts of sheep's wool caught on bushes. Since that practice required erratic movements and produced very little of value, it is now said that the act of idle daydreaming or purposeless thinking is *woolgathering*.

woolly

Wool is characterized by small fibers that produce a fuzzy outline. Figuratively, to be lacking in clarity or sharpness is to be *woolly*, as in "a *woolly* sound." Extended further, *woolly* means marked by mental confusion.

Worm

The Modern English word *worm* for a type of elongated soft-bodied animal goes back to Old English *wyrm* ("worm"), which is based on an Indo-European root meaning "to bend, turn, twist." The worm, then, is "the twister."

bookworm

Some insects live by eating books. Such a vermin is informally known as a bookworm. A person whose main interest in life is reading (figuratively devouring) books is also referred to as a *bookworm*.

can of worms

A situation that is likely to cause trouble or a sensitive topic that should be left alone is a *can of worms*. To bring about problems or to do something that has complex repercussions is *to open a can of worms*.

food for worms

A corpse or a carcass is *food for worms*.

worm

The worm has an ugly reputation for its crawling movement; its slimy appearance; and its slow, sometimes hidden, eating of other bodies, dead or alive. Because of the worm's disgusting reputation, a person who is hated or pitied is sometimes called a *worm*. A *worm* is also a sadness or a passion that seems to "eat" away a person's heart (as a worm eats a dead body). An object resembling a worm in appearance or action, such as a zigzag road, is a *worm*.

To move or crawl like a worm is *to worm*. To get something by being devious is *to worm* it out of someone else.

worm-eaten

Anything (such as wood) eaten by worms has an old, decayed look. Therefore, to be worn-out, old-fashioned, or decayed is to be *worm-eaten*.

a worm will turn

The worm is generally regarded as a weak, lowly creature. Yet people long ago noticed that if someone stepped on the rear part of a worm, the animal would turn as if to defend itself. That idea was expressed in the proverb *tread on a worm and it will turn*, that is, even a humble and weak person will fight back if he is abused too much. Today the expression is usually shortened to *a* (or *the*) *worm will* (or *may*) *turn*.

Zoo

The word *zoo* for a collection of living animals usually for public display is short for *zoological garden*, which was first applied to the Zoological Gardens in Regent's Park, London. *Zoo-* goes back to Greek *zoion* ("animal").

zoo

A place in which people are crowded together (as animals are generally crowded together in a zoo) is a *zoo*, such as a prison or a cafeteria. *Zoo* is also a derogatory name for any place or group, such as a despised family.

Part Two

Animal

The English word *animal* comes from Latin *animal* ("animal"), a derivative of *anima* ("air, breath, life, soul"), which is based on an Indo-European root meaning "to breathe."

animal

People often use the adjective *animal* to describe the physical or lower instincts in humans, as in "the *animal* nature in every person." The noun *animal* can refer to the human body itself, as in "The athlete is a magnificent *animal*." On the other hand, the word is sometimes used in an ugly sense to indicate an inhuman, beastlike person.

animal spirits

In the Middle Ages it was believed that human arteries carry not blood but gaseous spirits. Of the three kinds of spirits, the highest was called the *animal spirit*, after the Latin word *anima*. The *animal spirit* was thought to control the brain and the nerves. Later, of course, the word *animal* lost its "soul" meaning and came to refer to a living creature (other than plants), usually one lower than a human being. The expression *animal spirits*, however, continued to be used, but with an interesting twist. Earlier, people's healthy, vigorous energy and delight in life were presumed to come from their souls, that is, from their *animal spirits;* but later, with the loss of the "soul" sense of the word *animal,* the same expression, *animal spirits,* came to refer simply to the overflow of nervous energy and good health that humans share with young animals.

Animal Groups

The names of many animal groups have been extended to apply to groups of persons or things.

brace

Perhaps originally a cord with which dogs were coupled; later a pair of dogs, then a pair of any animal. *Brace* goes back to Latin *brachia* ("the two arms"), the plural of *brachium* ("arm"), itself from Greek *brachion* ("upper arm," originally "shorter," as opposed to the longer forearm), which is based on an Indo-European root meaning "short." Extended from the animal sense, *brace* means a pair of things or of humans.

brood

The young of certain animals, such as birds or fish; especially, a group of such animals hatched at one time and cared for by the same mother. *Brood* goes back to Old English *brod* ("offspring, brood"), which can be traced back to a Germanic root meaning "a warming, hatching, rearing of young," which in turn is based on an Indo-European root meaning "to boil." A set of children in one family or a group of a particular kind ("a new *brood* of filmmakers") is also a *brood*.

covey

A family of partridges or other game birds. *Covey* is

adapted from Old French *covee* ("a brood"), a derivative of the verb *cover* ("to hatch"), which goes back to Latin *cubare* ("to sit, incubate, hatch"), which is based on an Indo-European root meaning "to bend." Extended, *covey* means a family or a small group of persons or things.

drove

A large group of beasts, such as sheep or oxen, driven in a body. *Drove* goes back to Old English *draf* ("drove"), a derivative of the verb *drifan* ("to drive"), which is based on an Indo-European root meaning "to drive, push." According to the *Oxford English Dictionary*, the animal sense of *drove* was established before the word was extended to apply to a crowd of humans, especially when moving in concert.

flock

A group of animals, especially birds or goats or sheep, that live, travel, or feed together. *Flock* goes back to Old English *flocc* ("band of people," perhaps related to *folc*, "folk"). Today the use of *flock* for a group of people, especially one under the leadership of a single authority, is only as a transfer from the animal sense. A large number of anything can now be called a *flock*. Figuratively, Christianity is a *flock*, with Jesus as the Shepherd; and a Christian congregation is a *flock*, with the pastor as the shepherd (see *shepherd* under "Sheep" in Part One).

gaggle

A flock of geese, especially when not in flight. *Gaggle* comes from Middle English *gagyll* ("gaggle"), which derives from the imitative verb *gagelen* ("to cackle like a goose"). The animal sense of the word has extended to include any group of humans or objects bonded by some common element.

gam

A herd of whales or a social meeting of whalers at sea. *Gam* is of uncertain origin, but it may derive from English *gammon* ("idle or deceptive talk") or from Swedish and Norwegian dialectal *gams* ("loose conversation"). Extended, *gam* means any social visit.

herd

A group of animals of any kind feeding or traveling together. *Herd* goes back to Old English *heord* ("herd"), which is based on an Indo-European root meaning "herd." Extended, *herd* refers, usually disparagingly, to a large company of people. *The herd* is the common people. There can also be a *herd* of things, such as cars.

shoal

A large group of fish. *Shoal* derives from Middle Dutch *schole* ("multitude, troop, shoal of fishes"), which goes back to a Germanic source meaning "division," which is based on an Indo-European root meaning "to divide, cut." Extended, *shoal* names a crowd of humans.

stable

A building where horses are housed or allowed to stand. *Stable* comes from Old French *estable* ("stable"), itself from Latin *stabulum* ("stable," literally "standing place"), which is based on an Indo-European root meaning "to stand." *Stable* has extended by the following sequence of meanings: an establishment where racehorses are trained; the racehorses belonging to a particular owner; the personnel who keep and train racehorses; a group of athletes or performers under one management; and, finally, any group or collection.

swarm

A body of bees leaving an old hive for a new one. *Swarm* goes back to Old English *swearm* ("swarm"), which is based on an Indo-European root meaning "to buzz, hum, whisper." Transferred, *swarm* signifies a group of humans who leave one place to found a new community. Extended, the word refers to any large cluster of people or animals or things, especially when in motion.

Animal Homes

The names of many animal homes, whether made by humans or by the animals themselves, have been extended to apply to other dwellings or objects.

burrow

A hole dug in the ground by an animal, such as a fox or a rabbit, and used as a dwelling place by that animal. The form *burrow*, a variant of *borough*, goes back through Old English *burg* ("fortress") to a Germanic word meaning "hillfort" to an Indo-European root meaning "high." A small secluded human habitation is sometimes called a *burrow*.

cage

A place of confinement for birds and other animals. *Cage* is adopted from Old French *cage* ("cage"), itself from Latin *cavea* ("a hollow, hole, cave," hence "cage"), a derivative of the adjective *cavus* ("hollow"), which goes back to an Indo-European root meaning "to swell" and its derivatives meaning "a swelling, cavity, hole." Transferred, *cage* refers to a cell or an area for human prisoners. Any enclosure resembling a cage in form or purpose—such as a screen behind home plate in baseball, a style of dress, or a supporting framework in construction—is called a *cage*.

coop

Originally a basket, later a cage or pen of basketwork for confining poultry; now a poultry pen of any material. *Coop* goes back to Latin *cupa* ("cask, tub"), which is based on an Indo-European root meaning "hollow place, enclosing object." Extended, *coop* refers to any poorly made structure or confined area, for example, a jail. To confine is *to coop* (up).

den

The place of habitation of a wild animal. *Den* comes from Old English *denn* ("lair"), which is based on a Germanic or Indo-European root meaning "low ground, flattened place." *Den* has many extended meanings, such as a cavern (especially a hideout), a center of secret activity, a squalid dwelling, a secluded room, and a subdivision of a cub-scout pack.

hive

A structure for housing bees (especially honeybees), or the colony of bees themselves in the hive. *Hive* goes back to Old English *hyf* ("hive"), which is based on an Indo-European root meaning "to bend, curve, arch," whence "a round or hollow object." Extended, *hive* means a place swarming with active people or a crowd of such people.

kennel

A house for a dog or dogs. *Kennel* goes back to Latin *canis* ("dog"), which is based on an Indo-European root meaning "dog." Extended, *kennel* stands for a dwelling unfit for humans.

lair

A place where a wild animal lies down to rest, that is, a living place. *Lair* goes back to Old English *leger* ("lair"), which is based on an Indo-European root meaning "to lie, recline." *Lair* has extended its meaning to include a refuge or a hiding place for humans.

mew

Originally a cage for hawks while molting (formerly

known as "mewing"). *Mew* derives from Middle English *mewe* ("cage for molting hawks"), which goes back through the Old French noun *mue* ("a molting") to the Old French verb *muer* ("to molt") to Latin *mutare* ("to change") to an Indo-European root meaning "to change, go, move." A place for hiding or retirement is now known as a *mew*.

nest

A place where an animal, especially a bird, deposits its eggs or young. *Nest* comes from Old English *nest* ("nest"), which is based on a compound of the Indo-European roots *ni* ("down") and *sed* ("to sit"). A nest, then, is literally "a place to sit down." Extended from its animal sense, *nest* means any specific location, such as a snug resting place or a spot where something bad develops.

pen

A small enclosure for domestic animals. *Pen* comes from Old English *penn* ("pen for cattle"), which is related to *pinn* ("pin, peg") and goes back to an Indo-European root meaning "a projecting point." Extended, *pen* means any small place of confinement or storage.

perch

Originally any kind of pole or stick; now a horizontal bar for a bird to rest on. *Perch* goes back to Latin *pertica* ("pole"). From the bird-related sense of the word has come the idea of referring to a human resting place as a *perch*.

roost

A bird's resting place. *Roost* goes back to Old English *hrost* ("wooden framework of a roof, perch, roost"), which is based on an Indo-European root meaning "framework, timberwork." Extended from its bird-related sense, *roost* means any place for sitting, resting, or staying. To be in charge of a place (as a rooster controls the chicken roost) is *to rule the roost*. This is an Americanized version of the much older British expression *to rule the roast*, of obscure origin.

warren

Originally land enclosed and preserved for keeping and breeding animals; now specifically land where rabbits breed. *Warren* goes back to Old North French *warenne* ("game preserve"), which derives from a Germanic root meaning "to protect, guard," which in turn is based on an Indo-European root meaning "to cover." From the rabbit-related sense, *warren* has extended its meaning to include any human tenement or poor district as crowded and full of life as a rabbit's breeding ground.

Animal Locomotion

Some verbs referring to various kinds of animal locomotion have been extended to apply to other kinds of locomotion or conduct.

to amble

Of a horse, to move by lifting the feet in alternate pairs: first the two on one side, then the two on the other. The result is a smooth, easy pace. *To amble* goes back to Latin *ambulare* ("to walk"), which is based on an Indo-European root meaning "to wander, walk aimlessly." The verb has extended to humans. At first *to amble* meant simply to ride an ambling horse. Later came the figurative sense of to walk in an easy, leisurely motion.

to burrow

Of such small animals as a rabbit and a mole, to dig a hole in the ground, especially for hiding or dwelling. *To burrow* comes from the noun *burrow* (see *burrow* under "Animal Homes"). The verb has developed such extended senses relating to humans as to excavate, to progress in any manner suggestive of digging (such as "*to burrow* into the problem"), to conceal oneself as if in a burrow, and to snuggle.

to canter

Of a horse, to move at a moderate gallop, raising both of the forefeet simultaneously. *To canter* is short for the obsolete *to canterbury*, which goes back through the noun *canterbury* to the adjective *Canterbury* (in such phrases as *Canterbury pace, trot, gallop*), which ultimately derives from the name of the city of Canterbury, England, because of the supposed gait of the mounted pilgrims to the shrine of Saint Thomas à Becket in that city. Extended to humans, *to canter* means to move briskly, to lope.

to fly

Of winged creatures, to move through the air with wings. *To fly* goes back to Old English *fleogan* ("to fly"), which is based on an Indo-European root meaning "to move forward (by swimming, running, or flying)," which is an extension of another root meaning "to flow." *To fly* has developed a great many extensions. For example, it can refer to other things that move through the air, such as clouds, bullets, and planes. Anything that moves quickly—a person, an animal, a rumor—is said *to fly*. To vanish (as a mist often does) is *to fly*. Furthermore, one can tell someone else *to go fly* a kite, at which the offended party may well *fly* into a rage and *fly* at the first party's throat. On the other hand, they can amiably get together and *fly* high. One can also *fly* in the face of convention and *fly* the coop. There are no flies on the verb *to fly*.

to gallop

Of a horse, to go at a fast gait in which the animal is completely off the ground during each stride and in which the feet land in the following order: one hind foot, the diagonal biped along with the opposite hind foot, then the remaining forefoot. *To gallop* is adapted from Old French *galoper* ("to gallop"), a variant of Old North French *waloper* ("to gallop"), which goes back to Frankish unattested *walahlaupan* ("to run well"). Extended to humans or things or abstractions, *to gallop* means to go fast, as in "Time *galloped* by." The participial form *galloping* is commonly used, as in *"galloping* inflation."

to trot

Of a horse, to move at a gait between walking and running in which the legs move in diagonal pairs. *To trot* goes back to Old French *troter* ("to trot"), which comes from Old High German *trotton* ("to tread"), which is based on an Indo-European root meaning "to run, step." Extended to humans, *to trot* means to jog between a walk and a run, but it can also mean to move about briskly.

To trot out originally meant, and still means, to lead out and show off (a horse). In an extended sense, *to trot out* means to exhibit or show off (anything).

Animal-related Expressions

There are many common expressions that contain no actual animal words but that have animal-related origins. The following are some familiar examples.

a

The letter *a* can be traced back to an ancient Phoenician sign. The Phoenicians used it to represent the sound of a laryngeal consonant and called it *aleph* ("ox").

also-ran

A racing animal, such as a horse or a dog, that does not place in a competition is called an also-ran. Extended to humans, the same term can apply to a person who does not fare well in any kind of contest. Figuratively, a person of little or no importance in any sense is called an *also-ran*.

bag of tricks

In a fable by the French author Jean de La Fontaine (1621-95) occurs this sentence (in an 1841 translation): "But fox, in arts of siege well versed, Ransacked his bag of tricks accursed." From that passage has come the practice of referring to a stock of resources as a *bag of tricks*.

bait

At one time, there was in England a popular though

cruel sport of chaining or otherwise confining an animal (such as a badger, a bear, or a bull) and then having dogs attack it. The dogs were said to bait the animal (this sense of *to bait* goes back to Old Norse *beita*, "to cause to bite," based on *bita*, "to bite"). Thus, the sport was called badgerbaiting, bearbaiting, bullbaiting, and so on. Figuratively, among humans, to harass, nag, or tease is *to bait*.

As a noun, *bait* means food used to entice a prey. Figuratively, any lure or temptation is a *bait*.

bat one's eyes

To bat one's eyes means to wink them, especially in surprise or emotion. *To bat*, in this sense, comes from *to bate* referring to hawks and meaning to flap the wings wildly.

beat about the bush

Another popular sport in England was called batfowling, that is, hunting birds at night. One person would wake the birds by using a stick, or bat, to beat the bushes near the main flock. Someone else would attract the birds with a light and cause them to fly into a net held by one of the batfowlers. Today, then, to approach a subject indirectly or to avoid coming to the main point (as the batfowlers avoided actually hitting the flock of birds) is *to beat about* (or *around*) *the bush*.

bite

When a fish seizes or snaps at the bait of an angler, it is said to bite. Figuratively, among humans, to respond so as to be caught by a trick of any kind is *to bite*.

bite the hand that feeds one

A surly dog often snaps at the hand of a person offering it food. Thus, it is said that to act ungratefully is *to bite the hand that feeds one*.

blubber

Blubber is the fat of whales and other large marine mammals. Excessive fat on humans has also come to be called *blubber*.

bone of contention

A bone often causes a fight between dogs. Hence, the simple word *bone*, often in the phrase *to cast a bone between*, was at one time used to mean something that causes strife. Today anything that creates a conflict or an argument is more specifically called a *bone of contention*.

bone to pick

A dog often spends a great deal of time and effort chewing on a bone. Therefore, anything that occupies a person was once called a *bone to pick*. The same phrase has also meant a difficulty to solve. Today a grievance or a point of contention is a *bone to pick*.

breed

The basic sense of the verb *to breed*, to produce (offspring), applies equally to humans and to animals. But according to the *Oxford English Dictionary*, there is at least one sense in which an earlier animal-related meaning of the word has been extended to humans. This is the sense of to rear (animals) so as to develop their physical qualities or intelligence. Extended to humans, this sense means to bring up, nurture, train, as in the familiar phrase *born and bred* (in the country, for example).

The noun *breed* in the sense of lineage, according to the *Oxford English Dictionary*, was first applied to animals and then to humans.

bridle

When the reins on a horse are abruptly pulled, the animal will react with a sharp upward movement of its head. The reins are part of the bridle. Therefore, among humans, to tuck in the chin and throw back the head as in protest or vanity or scorn is *to bridle*. More broadly, to give any evidence of hostility is *to bridle*.

brood

It is said of a bird that to sit on, or to hatch, eggs is to brood. And to protect young birds by covering with the wings is also to brood. Among humans, then, to sit quietly and thoughtfully or to worry is *to brood.*

browse

Tender young shoots, twigs, and leaves on trees and shrubs are called browse. When casually nibbling on such material, an animal is said to browse. The idea of browsing has been figuratively applied to humans: to inspect something in a leisurely way is *to browse. To browse* at a library means to "nibble" at the books.

bury one's head in the sand

When an ostrich is faced with danger, it will run away or, if fatigued or cornered, kick its pursuer violently. Nevertheless, there is an old false belief that an ostrich will bury its head in the sand to avoid danger. That belief is based on the bird's habit of lowering its long neck to avoid detection while hatching or protecting its young. It is figuratively said that to avoid reality or to ignore facts is *to bury one's head in the sand.*

busman's holdiay

A *busman's holiday* is a day off from work spent in an activity closely resembling one's usual occupation. The origin of this expression is said to lie in the habits of nineteenth-century British drivers of horse-drawn omnibuses. On their days off, the drivers would return to the stables to make certain that their horses were being treated properly by the relief drivers. Some regular drivers would even ride all day as passengers on their own buses to watch over their horses and to keep the relief drivers company.

by a nose

In horseracing, the nose of a horse is a literal indicator of the distance of a narrow victory. Among humans, therefore, to win by an extremely narrow margin in any endeavor (such as an election) is to win *by a nose.*

c

The letter *c* can be traced back to an ancient Phoenician

sign. The Phoenicians used it to represent our *g* sound and called it *gimel* ("camel"). (See also *g* below.)

champ at the bit

When a horse is anxious to get moving, it will chew on the bit (part of the bridle) in its mouth. Figuratively, among humans, to show impatience is *to champ* (or *chafe*) *at the bit.*

cinch

A cinch is a strong band or strap that encircles the body of an animal to fasten a pack or a saddle on its back. Any tight grip, then, is a *cinch*. The idea of tightness implies certitude, so that a certainty or a thing done with ease is also a *cinch*.

clutch

Clutch, originally meaning the claw of a beast, has extended to include the familiar modern meanings: a grasping hand, an unrelenting control or power, a machinery device (such as that on a car), a tense situation.

come to the end of one's rope

An animal tied to a stake can graze only as far as the rope will go. Sometimes an animal trying to reach beyond the end of the rope will stretch and strain and practically choke itself to death. But, of course, the animal usually fails and gets nothing for the effort but frustration and exhaustion. Figuratively, among humans, to reach the limit of one's energy or ability is *to come to* (or *be at*) *the end of one's rope* (or *tether*).

constable

In medieval France, the head groom of a stable was called, in Late Latin, *comes stabuli* ("officer of the stable"). At that time, horses were extremely valuable for their uses in transportation and in war. Being in charge of the horses was an important job. Hence, *comes stabuli* came to refer to a high officer of a royal or noble household, or to a high military officer. Those last two senses were taken into English through the Old French form *conestable*. The present form, *constable*, refers to any of various public officers of the peace. In England, a policeman is a *constable*. (Compare *marshal* under "Animals Hidden in Words.")

curry

One of the steps in currying, or dressing, a tanned animal hide is to beat it. Hence, to beat a man is *to curry* him.

Favel is an obsolete English word for a fallow-colored, or chestnut, horse. Such a horse is proverbial as a symbol of dishonesty. That idea originated in, or was early incorporated in, a 1310 French book called *Roman de Fauvel*. From *Roman de Fauvel* comes the English expression *to curry Favel/favel* (translated from Old French *estriller Fauvel/fauvel*), literally meaning to rub or smooth down the chestnut horse and figuratively meaning to seek to gain favor by flattery or fawning. By folk etymology, *to curry favel* has become *to curry favor*.

decoy

Decoy originally meant a pond covered with network in such a way as to capture fowl that were lured in (*decoy* coming from Dutch *de kooi*, literally "the cage," actually "the enclosure for trapping fowl"). *Decoy* has since come to refer to a bird (real or artificial) that lures others into a position for being shot. That sense has been extended, so that a person or a thing used to entice others into any kind of a trap is called a *decoy*.

desert a sinking ship

In ancient times, people thought that rats had some special association with human souls. It was widely believed that rats often warned their human neighbors of impending disaster or death. If rats suddenly left a house, for example, people feared that the house would collapse or that a person living there would have a terrible misfortune. And if rats suddenly left a ship just before it sailed, sailors feared that the ship was doomed to sink on its next voyage. Therefore, among humans, to run away during a time of trouble and let others face a bad situation is (like the rats) *to desert a sinking ship*.

earmark

To earmark a domestic animal is to mark its ear as a sign of ownership or identity. Hence, to mark anything in a distinguishing way is *to earmark* it. Further extended, *to earmark* means to designate for a specific use, as in "The money is *earmarked* for a new house."

eat humble pie

Umbles are the internal organs (heart, liver, and so on) of an animal, especially a deer. A variant spelling of *umbles* is *humbles*. People used to make a dish called humble pie, a pie made of umbles. The pie was thought to be an inferior food. To eat humble pie was to demonstrate one's modest circumstances. Because of that literal sense of *humble pie* and because of a confusion with, or a consciously humorous reference to, the unrelated word *humble* meaning meek or lowly, people say that to be submissive or apologetic or humiliated is *to eat humble pie*.

fawn

Originally referring only to animals, especially dogs, *to fawn* means to show delight or affection, as by licking and tail-wagging. Extended to humans, *to fawn* means to court favor by a servile, groveling manner.

fledge

Fledge is an obsolete English adjective meaning fit (with feathers) to fly. From that sense of the word has come the present verb *to fledge*, meaning to acquire large enough feathers for flight. This verb is sometimes applied to humans and means to attain a state of competence characteristic of maturity. More often, though, it is seen in the form of a participle, as in "She is a full-*fledged* pilot."

flutter

The first, and long obsolete, meaning of *to flutter* was to float to and fro on waves. The primary modern meaning refers especially to birds and means to flap the wings rapidly. The verb has extended its meaning, so that anything moving in short, quick motions—such as water, a flame, or an agitated heart—can be said *to flutter*. The sense has further extended to refer to human conduct, so that to move about or behave in an agitated, aimless manner is *to flutter*.

fly the coop

A coop is a poultry pen. By extension, *coop* means any place of confinement. To flee such a place is *to fly the coop*. (See also *coop* under "Animal Homes" and *to fly* under "Animal Locomotion.")

foot-in-mouth disease

Foot-and-mouth (or hoof-and-mouth) disease is an acute, contagious disease of hoofed animals. A play has been made on the animal-related *foot-and-mouth disease* and the common human-related expression *to put one's foot in one's mouth*, so that, among humans, to say or do the wrong thing is to have *foot-in-mouth disease*.

g

The letter *g* can be traced back to an ancient Phoenician sign. The Phoenicians used it to represent our own *g* sound and called it *gimel* ("camel"). (See also *c* above.)

get a rise out of one

In angling, to lure a fish up to the surface to take a fly or a bait is to get a rise out of the fish. According to the *Oxford English Dictionary*, it was from that angling image that people derived the idea of saying that to provoke an angry reaction from one (that is, to lure one's temper to the surface) is *to get a rise out of one*.

get one's back up

An angry cat will arch its back. Therefore, to become angry is *to get one's back up*.

get up on one's hind legs

When angered, a horse will rise up on its hind legs. Hence, among humans, to become angry is *to get* (or *rear*) *up on one's hind legs*.

Some animals, such as bears, will rise up on their hind legs to fight. Hence, among humans, to stand up and face adversity is *to stand up on one's hind legs.*

get wind of

Many animals have a keen sense of smell. When the wind is blowing in a favorable direction, the animals can detect the scents of nearby persons or other animals. Figuratively, among humans, to get advanced knowledge of something is *to get wind of* it.

groom

To attend to the cleaning of an animal, especially a horse, is to groom it. Extended to humans or to things, *to groom* them means to give them a neat appearance. Further extended, *to groom* people means to prepare them for something (such as politics); and to refine something (such as language) is *to groom* it.

halter

A halter is a device of rope or leather straps by which an animal can be led or secured. Transferred to humans, *halter* means a rope with a noose for execution by hanging. *Halter* also means execution itself. A garment that covers the breast of a woman or a girl and that leaves the shoulders, arms, and back bare is called a *halter.*

To hamper or restrain is *to halter.*

hands down

In nineteenth-century horseracing, the phrase *to win hands down* referred to the jockey dropping his hands and relaxing his hold on the reins when victory appeared certain. Today to do anything easily or without question is to do it *hands down.*

hark back

The basic meaning of the verb *to hark* is to pay close attention. In hunting, the noun *hark* is a call of attention and incitement to the hounds on the scent of an animal. Hounds are said to hark back when they return along the course to regain a lost scent. Figuratively, among humans, to return to some earlier topic or circumstance is *to hark back.*

harness

A harness is the gear other than a yoke of a draft animal. Figuratively, among humans, the routine of regular work is a *harness,* as in "to get back into *harness* after an illness" and "to work in *harness* with others." A common way of saying to die in the midst of work is *to die in harness.*

hatch

When a hen sits on an egg until the chick breaks out of the shell, the hen is said to hatch the chick. Among humans, therefore, to originate anything, especially in secret, is *to hatch* it.

hellbent for leather

Since the early 1800s, *hellbent* has meant recklessly determined. Later came *hellbent* (or *hell*) *for leather,* referring to riding on horseback (*leather* being metonymic for "saddle") and meaning galloping at breakneck speed or, extended, simply moving very quickly. Today *leather* is usually dropped from the expression, but *hellbent* retains not only its original sense of recklessly determined but also the horse-related sense of moving at full speed.

herd

As an intransitive verb, *to herd* refers to animals and means to go in a herd. Extended derisively to humans, the verb means to assemble or move in a group. As a transitive verb, *to herd* refers to the keeper of an animal herd and means to keep (the animals) together. Applied contemptuously to humans, *to herd* means to gather or lead (people as a herd).

hive

To store up (anything), as honeybees store up (honey), is *to hive* (something). To reside in close quarters, as bees do, is *to hive.*

Hobson's choice

Tobias (or Thomas) Hobson was an English liveryman who lived in the late 1500s and the early 1600s. He was known for forcing his customers to take the horse nearest the door or none at all. Therefore, an apparently free choice when there is no real alternative is a *Hobson's choice.*

hold out the olive branch

The olive branch was a symbol of peace in many parts of the ancient world, such as Greece and Rome. But the modern use of the symbol has probably derived most directly from a reference to it in the biblical story of Noah (Genesis 8:11): "And the dove came in to him in the evening; and lo, in her mouth was an olive leaf pluckt off; so Noah knew that the waters were abated from off the earth." Figuratively, anything offered as a token of peace is an *olive branch,* and to offer any sign of goodwill or improved conditions (as the dove did to Noah) is *to hold out the olive branch.*

hook

A certain kind of hook, a fishhook, is made to catch a fish. Figuratively, something by which a person is attracted and caught is a *hook.* To catch a person is *to hook* him.

To be ensnared, in the power of someone, or attached to some activity is to be *on the hook.* To be out of a difficult situation is to be *off the hook.*

A hungry fish might swallow not only a fisherman's bait but also the fishhook, some line, and the lead sinker as well. Hence, the phrase *hook, line, and sinker* has come to mean entirely, completely. In particular, one can say that a gullible person completely duped has swallowed some false or foolish idea *hook, line, and sinker.*

hover

In its original reference to winged creatures, *to hover* means to suspend in midair over a spot by flapping the wings, especially when preparing to swoop. Extended, *to hover* applies to any object that hangs over a place, such as a cloud that seems stationary. A person or an animal that moves to and fro near a place is said *to hover*. To be in a state of uncertainty or irresolution—that is, to be "suspended" over a decision before "swooping" to take it—is *to hover*.

hullabaloo

Halloo is an old British exclamation used to incite dogs to the chase during a hunt. *Halloo* was reduplicated and rhymed into *halloo-baloo*, which, in allusion to the turmoil of the hunt, stood for any noisy confusion. *Halloo-baloo* is now spelled *hullabaloo*.

in one's hair

Hair lice irritate the scalp. Therefore, to pester or annoy one irritatingly is, like the lice, to be *in one's hair*.

in the bag

When something is certain to happen, it is said to be *in the bag*. *Bag* is generally thought to be short for *gamebag*, the expression alluding to game that has been killed, or is certain to be killed, and put into the bag. According to the *Oxford English Dictionary* (1972 supplement), the expression originated in Australia and New Zealand about 1900 to describe a horse set to lose a race. Somewhat later, in general English, to be taken prisoner was *to be put in the bag*. In the United States, *in the bag* dates from the 1920s and in early quotations describes an expected outcome in such sports as racing and boxing.

kennel

Referring originally only to dogs, *to kennel* means to dwell in a kennel. Extended to humans, *to kennel* means to provide with a living place unfit for people. It also means to seek lodging in a secluded location. Further extended, *to kennel* means to confine or restrain.

kick over the traces

Traces are the straps or chains connecting a harnessed draft animal to the vehicle it is pulling. A horse will sometimes get a leg over the traces so as to kick more freely. Figuratively, among humans, to throw off restraint or authority—that is, to show independence—is *to kick over the traces*.

land on one's feet

No matter how a cat falls, it always seems to land safely on its feet. That observation has long been applied figuratively to humans, so that to remain safe or successful after going through a hardship is *to land on one's feet* (or *legs*).

lead by the nose

Animals have long been literally led by the nose, either by bit and bridle (as with horses and donkeys) or by a ring in the nostrils (as with bears, buffaloes, and camels). Since ancient times, the expression *to lead by the nose* has been figuratively applied to humans who are so foolish or docile that they need to be guided. It was, for example, used in ancient Greece. But the modern use of the expression probably derives most directly from a reference in the Bible (Isaiah 37:29): "Because thy rage against me, and thy tumult, is come up into mine ears, therefore will I put my hook in thy nose, and my bridle in thy lips, and I will turn thee back by the way by which thou camest."

leash

A leash is a line for holding an animal. In sporting language, a leash is a set of three of an animal, as of deer, foxes, hares, or hounds. Now a set of three of anything can be called a *leash*.

A horse or a dog is commonly controlled by being tied to a leash. That idea has been figuratively transferred to humans, so that to have control over (someone, something) is *to hold* (or *have*) (someone, something) *in leash*.

An animal anxious to move faster will commonly run out to the end of its leash and literally pull its owner along. That idea has been figuratively applied to humans, so that to be anxious to do more than one is allowed is *to strain at the leash*.

lick into shape

In the Middle Ages, it was widely believed that a baby

bear is born as a shapeless mass and that the mother has to lick the object with her tongue until the blob is molded into the proper shape for a little bear cub. Today, among humans, to make presentable, such as to bring up (children) well, is *to lick into shape.*

litter

The original, now obsolete, sense of the noun *litter* was a bed (*litter* goes back to Latin *lectus,* "bed"). From that sense has come *litter* meaning the material, such as straw, serving as bedding for animals. The transitive verb *to litter* has the primary sense of to furnish (an animal) with litter for a bed. Since *to litter* means to cover (the floor) with loose material for an animal bed, the verb has come to mean to scatter (things) in disorder, without reference to a bed. The material thus scattered is *litter.*

long in the tooth

As a horse ages, its gums recede, showing the roots of the teeth and making the teeth seem longer. Figuratively, among humans, to be old is to be *long in the tooth.*

mad as a hatter

(As) mad as a hatter means completely mad, or crazy. The origin of this expression is uncertain, but there are two common explanations. One is that the chemicals used in making felt hats can cause a hat worker to develop a nervous illness that others mistake for insanity.

Another explanation is that *hatter* is a variation of Old English *atter* ("poison") or of Modern English *adder,* the name of a poisonous snake whose bite was thought to cause insanity. *(As) mad as a hatter,* then, could be a shortened corruption of the assumed expression *(as) mad as a person bitten by an adder.* Or since *atter* and *adder* were associated with the causing of insanity, they may, in the language of the folk, have become symbols of insanity itself, so that *(as) mad as a hatter* could be a shortened version of *(as) mad as a mad adder.* Some authorities, however, believe that *mad* here originally meant angry, so that *(as) mad as a hatter* meant as angry or malicious as a striking adder. Soon, though, *mad* took on the current sense of crazy.

mew

In its original reference to hawks, *to mew* meant to put (a hawk) into a "mew," a cage, at molting time. Now extended to humans, *to mew* means to shut up, confine. It is often used with *up*.

n

The letter *n* can be traced back to an ancient Phoenician sign. The Phoenicians used it to represent our own *n* sound and called it *nun* ("fish").

neck and neck

In horseracing, horses that are running close together, with neither gaining the advantage, are said to be neck and neck. This idea has been figuratively applied to humans, so that to be even or equal in any kind of competition is to be *neck and neck.*

nest, nestle

To nest originally refers to birds and other animals and means to make or occupy a nest. Extended to humans, *to nest* means to settle as if in a nest, so that to be established or comfortably placed is to be *nested.* The verb can also be applied to things or abstracts, as in "Love *nested* in his heart."

From *nest* comes *nestle.* Applied to birds, *to nestle* means to build or have a nest. Extended to humans, *to nestle* means to settle comfortably or to lie in an inconspicuous or sheltered manner.

off one's feed

When an animal, especially a horse, loses its appetite, as from illness, it is said to be off its feed. Transferred to humans, to be *off one's feed* has the same meaning. The expression has also been extended to include emotional as well as physical troubles, so that to be depressed is to be *off one's feed.*

off the hook

If a hooked fish manages to escape, it has obviously been

freed from a perilous situation. Figuratively, among humans, to be rid of a difficult situation or responsibility is to be *off the hook*.

one fell swoop

A bird of prey usually attacks in one sudden, savage descent. Such a move is characterized by the phrase *one fell swoop*, in which *fell* means fierce and *swoop* means a sudden (downward) attack. The expression has been figuratively transferred to humans, so that to do something at a single stroke or all at once is to do it at *one fell swoop*.

open season

A period when various types of game are legitimate quarry is called an open season. Therefore, a time when a person or an idea is particularly subject to attack is an *open season*.

pastor, pastoral, pasture, pester, repast

Several English words go back to Latin *pascere* ("to graze, feed," originally in reference to animals). For example, English *pastor* originally means a shepherd; extended, it means a minister. *Pastoral* originally means of a shepherd; extended, it means of a minister, of the country, and so on. *Pasture* has gone from meaning the action of feeding or grazing (said of animals) to the land itself for grazing. *To pester* does not have an animal-related origin in English, but it probably comes from Old French *empestrer* ("to entangle, hobble," originally "to tether [a grazing horse]"), which in turn goes back to Latin *pascere*. *Repast*, like *to pester*, does not have an animal-related origin in English; however, like the other words in this group, it is based on a Latin word, *pascere*, with an animal-related origin.

peck

In its original reference to birds, *to peck* means to strike, or to pick up food, with the beak. Extended to humans, *to peck* has developed such meanings as to strike with repeated small movements and to give a quick, casual kiss. *To peck at* means to eat sparingly or to criticize constantly.

pecking order

A flock of poultry usually lives in a hierarchy in which one member of the flock can peck another without the second one pecking back. In turn, the first submits to pecking by one of higher rank. And so on. This hierarchy is known as a pecking order. Human organizations have similar levels of power (determined by aggressive awareness of such factors as rank and income), figuratively called a *pecking order*.

perch

In its original reference to birds, *to perch* means to rest on a perch. Extended to humans and to things, *to perch* means to rest on something like a perch.

pipe

An imitative Indo-European root meaning "to peep" (like a bird) is the basis of Latin *pipare* ("to peep, chirp"). *Pipare* eventually yields the English noun *pipe* (meaning a musical tube, hence other tubular devices) and the verb *to pipe* (meaning to play on a pipe, hence to produce other sounds).

pitted against

To set animals, especially gamecocks, into a pit to fight each other is to pit them. From that practice has come the idea of saying that, among humans, to be set in opposition to is to be *pitted against*.

potshot

In hunting, a potshot is a shot taken at random or at an easy target, so called because such a shot is thought to be unsportsmanlike and suited only for one whose object is to fill his cooking pot. Figuratively, a critical remark lacking forethought is a *potshot*.

preen

To preen originally refers to a bird and means to trim (the feathers) with the beak. Extended to humans, *to preen* means to dress or smooth (oneself) up. Figuratively, *to preen* means to pride or congratulate (oneself).

prick up one's ears

Sometimes an animal, such as a horse, will raise its ears when it is excited. Therefore, among humans, it is said that to become alert is *to prick up one's ears.*

pull chestnuts out of the fire

In a fable, a monkey, to avoid burning his own hands, used a cat's paw to extract roasting chestnuts from a fire (see *cat's paw* under "Cat" in Part One). Hence, it is said of a duped person that to be pressed into doing someone's dangerous or unpleasant task is *to pull* (someone's) *chestnuts out of the fire.*

put one through one's paces

Paces are training steps, or gaits, of a horse. A horse that is put through its paces is required to display its full range of training. Therefore, among humans, to test one's ability to the utmost is *to put one through one's paces.*

put on the feed bag

A feed bag is a nose bag, that is, a bag of food suspended under a horse's nose so that the animal can eat. Jocularly, among humans, to begin eating is *to put on the feed bag.*

put out to pasture

Some animals, such as workhorses, in old age or in poor health are taken away from their work and literally put out to pasture, that is, to lazily graze their lives away. Among humans, then, to be forcibly retired is *to be put out to pasture.*

q

The letter *q* can be traced back to an ancient Phoenician sign. The Phoenicians used it to represent a sound not found in English or in any other Indo-European language. They called it *qoph* ("monkey").

quid

Quid stands for a cut or wad of something (usually

tobacco) chewable. The word is a variant of *cud*, which refers to a ruminating animal's food (see "Cud" in Part One).

ramp, rampage, rampant

To ramp comes from Old French *ramper* ("to crawl, climb"). In English, the word quickly developed a special reference to animals, real or as depicted in heraldry: to rise up on the hind legs (as if climbing), hence to assume a threatening posture (said especially of lions). That sense of the verb has been extended to humans, so that to threaten with arms raised or, figuratively, simply to act furiously is *to ramp*.

Evolving from the verb *to ramp* is the noun *rampage*, as in "to go on a *rampage*," meaning to fly into reckless, destructive, or violent behavior.

To ramp also yields the adjective *rampant*, meaning (of an animal) standing on the hind legs. Extended, *rampant* means without restraint. Further extended, it means widespread.

rein

A rein is a strap by which a rider or driver can control an animal. Figuratively, any means of guiding or controlling is a *rein*, as in "the *reins* of government." Any restraining influence can be called a *rein*.

To slow down or stop is *to draw rein* or *to draw in the reins*. To allow full freedom is *to give (the) rein(s) to* or *to give full* (or *free*) *rein to*. To check, control, or restrain is *to keep a rein on*.

ride

According to the *Oxford English Dictionary*, the verb *to ride* originally means to sit on and be carried by an animal. The verb now means to be carried in or on any kind of conveyance.

ride for a fall

A reckless rider of an animal is liable to be thrown off. Figuratively, to invite trouble or misfortune by any kind of reckless conduct is *to ride for a fall*. This is an animal-related way of expressing the same idea found in the Bible

(Proverbs 16:18): "Pride goeth before destruction, and an haughty spirit before a fall."

ride herd on

Cattle are controlled and driven by horseback riders prodding the animals along the edge of the herd. That idea has been figuratively applied to humans, so that to dominate, oppress, or (more mildly) supervise is *to ride herd on*.

ride roughshod over

A horse having shoes with projecting points is said to be roughshod. The projections help prevent the horse from slipping. But the appearance of the shoes is fearsome, especially to a person being charged by such a horse. It is figuratively said, then, that to domineer or act violently toward is *to ride roughshod over*.

road

Road, in its Old English spelling of *rad* and its Middle English spelling of *rode*, originally meant the act of riding on horseback. From that sense has come the modern *road*, meaning an open way for the passage of animals, persons, and vehicles.

roost

To roost originally refers to birds and means to settle on a perch for rest or sleep. Extended to humans, *to roost* means to seat oneself, to make one's abode, or to pass the night. (See *chickens always come home to roost* under "Chicken" in Part One.)

root

It is said of some animals, particularly swine, that to turn up or dig in the earth for food is to root. That original sense of the intransitive verb has been figuratively extended to humans, so that to poke about is *to root*. As a transitive verb, *to root (out)* has the extended sense of to discover and bring to light, as in *"to root (out)* the evil."

To root meaning to cheer or support may come from the above word. Or it may have another animal-related origin, being perhaps an alteration of the British dialectal verb *to rout*, that is, to bellow (said of cattle).

rope in

Cattle need to be roped and held for certain purposes, such as branding. Among humans, then, to draw into a plan by force or deception is *to rope in*.

round up, roundup

To round up cattle is to ride around the herd and drive the animals into an enclosure. Thus, to collect (scattered persons or things) is *to round* (them) *up*. The act of rounding up, in the animal sense or the extended sense, is a *roundup*.

rouse

Rouse was originally a technical term in hawking. *To rouse* referred to a hawk and meant to shake the feathers (of itself). From that reflexive sense, the verb extended to mean to cause (game) to break from cover—presumably by "shaking" them up. Soon the word was used figuratively, as in *"to rouse* the muse." The expression has further extended, so that today to awaken (literally or figuratively) or stimulate or provoke is *to rouse*.

roust

To roust is an alteration of *to rouse* (see *rouse* above) and means to rout (see *rout* below), especially out of bed.

rout

Rout is a variant of *root* (see *root* above). *To rout* refers to swine and means to use the snout to turn up the earth searching for food. Among humans, it is said that to poke about or rummage is *to rout*. To fetch out of bed, to expel by force, and to uncover and bring to light are further extensions of *to rout*.

run counter to

In hunting, the expression *to hunt* (or *run* or *go*) *counter* means to go in a direction opposite to that which the game has taken. Figuratively, *to run* (or *go* or *act*) *counter to* means to be contrary to or in opposition to.

runner-up

The term *runner-up* originally refers to a dog that takes

second place in a dog race. Today the second-place finisher in any kind of activity is a *runner-up.*

saddle

The original sense of *saddle* is a seat for the rider of an animal. Any similar seat is therefore called a *saddle,* such as that on a bicycle or a tractor. Something resembling a saddle in shape or position is a *saddle.* Figuratively, *in the saddle* means in control. To lose control or composure is to become *unsaddled.*

To place under a burden, as a horse is burdened with a saddle, is *to saddle,* usually *to saddle with,* as in "They *saddled* themselves *with* many debts."

shoo-in

Shoo is an echoic interjection used to frighten away an animal. The interjection has become the transitive verb *to shoo,* meaning to scare or drive away (usually an animal) by, or as if by, crying *shoo. To shoo in* means to drive (usually an animal) into an enclosure. Hence, a *shoo-in* is someone or something expected to win easily, as if shooed into the winner's position by an omnipotent force.

show one's teeth

Some animals, such as dogs, pull back their lips and expose their teeth when preparing to bite or attack. Figuratively, among humans, to express a readiness for fighting or to behave in a threatening way is *to show one's teeth.*

slow and steady wins the race

In Aesop's fable "The Hare and the Tortoise," the hare was so certain of victory in a race with the tortoise that it stopped to nap. The tortoise plodded steadily on and won the race. Today, then, a way of saying that careful, constant effort will accomplish more than hurried, sporadic effort will is *slow and steady wins the race.*

small fry

Fry originally meant human offspring. But that sense of the word has, according to the *Oxford English Dictionary,* become obsolete except as a transfer from the currently primary sense of the word: the young of fish or of other animals produced in large numbers, such as bees and frogs. Members of any group or class are now called *fry*. In particular, young or insignificant beings are called *small fry*.

snare

A snare is a device consisting of a noose (*snare* coming from Old Norse *snara*, "noose") for capturing wild animals or birds. Thus, anything by which a person is entangled or impeded has come to be called a *snare*. Something deceptively attractive is also a *snare*.

To entrap (literally an animal, figuratively a human) is *to snare*.

sour grapes

In one of the fables ascribed to Aesop, a fox who could not reach a bunch of grapes that he desired consoled himself by saying that the fruit was probably sour anyway. Disparagement of something desired but unattainable is now called *sour grapes*.

spar

In reference to gamecocks, the verb *to spar* means to fight, specifically to strike with the feet or spurs. That sense has been extended to human boxers, so that to practice boxing is *to spar*. Figuratively, to contest in words, to engage in a military skirmish, or to stall is *to spar*.

spur

The original meaning of the word *spur* is a sharp device for poking and urging on a horse. The word has extended its meaning to include such senses as any goad to action, something suggesting a spur (such as a projecting branch of a tree, a sharp projection on a rooster's leg, or a gaff for a gamecock), a ridge that extends laterally from a mountain, and a short wooden brace of a post.

The original meaning of *to spur* is to urge (a horse) on with spurs. Extended, *to spur* means to incite (a person or a thing) to action. It often takes the form *to spur on*.

To do something on a sudden impulse is to do it, as a horse reacts to a sudden kick by a spur, *on the spur of the moment.*

To urge forward, as a rider uses spurs to kick a horse into action, is *to set* (or *put*) *spurs to.*

In the Middle Ages, a squire went into battle with silver spurs, while a knight wore gilt spurs. If a squire performed courageously in battle, he would be rewarded with a knighthood and would be presented with a pair of gilt spurs as a symbol of his achievement. Figuratively, then, to attain a distinction or to make a reputation is *to win one's spurs.*

stamping ground

A stamping ground is a place where animals, especially horses, customarily gather to stamp. Therefore, a place where people are or were accustomed to go is called their *(old) stamping ground.*

stand the gaff

To stand the gaff means to endure criticism, ridicule, or punishment. *Gaff* may come from Scottish *gaff* ("loud, rude talk"), but some sources say that the word may refer to the steel spurs worn by fighting cocks.

sting

Originally referring to such animals as wasps, scorpions, and snakes, *to sting* means to pierce or wound with a point. Extended, *to sting* means to cause a sharp pain, such as that caused by a bullet or a cold wind. Figuratively, to cause mental suffering is *to sting.* And to cheat, especially by overcharging, is *to sting.*

stride

The regular or uniform movement of a horse in a race is its stride. Among humans, then, one's most effective natural pace (in any activity) or the height of one's activity is one's *stride,* commonly used in the expressions *to get into one's stride* and *to do* (something) *in one's own stride.*

When a horse clears an obstacle, the animal is said to have taken the obstacle in its stride. That idea has been figuratively transferred to humans, so that to proceed in the face of a problem without changing one's normal pace or sense of equilibrium is *to take in one's stride.*

strike a bargain

In ancient Rome, the Latin verb *ferire* had the basic meaning of "to strike"; it also had extensions meaning "to kill by striking" and "to kill (any animal) as a sacrifice" for the purpose of making a solemn commitment. The word was used in the common expression *ferire foedus*, meaning "to make an agreement," literally "to strike (that is, to solemnly commit oneself to, as if sacrificing an animal to a deity) an agreement." *Ferire foedus* and the early English expression *to strike* (shake) *hands* are the sources of the modern expression *to strike a bargain*, meaning to make an agreement.

swarm

In its original reference to bees, *to swarm* means to gather together and leave the hive to start a new colony. Extended to humans, *to swarm* means to move or assemble in a crowd.

tacky

An inferior horse is called, especially in the South, a tacky. Extended, *tacky*, in the same region, means a poor white. Today the word is commonly used as an adjective: something shabby or lacking in good taste is *tacky*.

take the bit between one's teeth

To lessen the discomfort of a bit (the mouthpiece of a bridle), a horse will take the bit in its teeth. Therefore, it is often said of humans that to rebel or to take charge of one's own life is *to take the bit between* (or *in*) *one's teeth.*

team

From *team* meaning a set of draft animals comes *team* meaning a group of persons organized for some purpose.

trammel

The original meaning of the word *trammel* (based on Latin *tres*, "three," plus *macula*, "mesh") is a three-layered net for catching fish. Figuratively, anything that confines or restrains is a *trammel*. To impede or to confine is *to trammel*. The word is commonly found in the participial form *untrammeled*, meaning unrestrained.

trap

A trap is originally a device for catching game or other animals. The word *trap* has developed many transferred and figurative senses. For example, something by which a person is caught or stopped (literally or figuratively) unawares is a *trap*.

tunnel

The English word *tunnel* is adapted from Old French *tonel* ("tun, cask"), a diminutive of *tonne* ("tun"). The early English use of the word was in reference to the tubelike shape of a small tun; specifically, a tunnel was a conical net for catching game. From that animal-related use of the word have come all of the familiar modern extensions: tube, well, covered passageway, burrow.

under one's skin

Mites, ticks, and some other insects embed themselves under the skin of victims and cause itching and irritation. Thus, to be irritated or deeply affected by someone or something is to have the person or thing *under one's skin*.

up a tree

To be trapped in a bad situation (as an animal may be trapped in a tree by hunting dogs) is to be *up a tree*.

viscosity, viscous

In ancient Latin, *viscum* is originally "mistletoe." The Romans used mistletoe to make birdlime; therefore, *viscum* is extended to mean "birdlime." *Viscum* yields the Latin adjective *viscosus* ("full of birdlime, sticky"), which becomes English *viscous* and *viscosity*.

walkover

It is said of a racehorse that to go over a course at a walking pace so as to be judged the winner in a race in which there is no opposition is to walk over (the course). Such a "race" is a walkover. Among humans, then, a one-sided contest or something easily done is called a *walkover*.

wallop

The English verb *to wallop* is originally a form of the verb *to gallop* (Middle English *walopen*, "to gallop," coming from Old North French *waloper*, "to gallop"; see also *to gallop* under "Animal Locomotion"). The word has evolved many extensions based on the general suggestion of violent, noisy movements (like those of a galloping horse). As an intransitive verb, *to wallop* means to beat soundly, to hit with a hard blow, or to defeat thoroughly. The noun *wallop* stands for a hard punch, the ability to deliver such a punch, or an emotional impact.

wampum

North American Indians used to polish animal shells, string them together, and use them as money, pledges, and ornaments. Algonquian Indians called the results (in one of many recorded spellings) *wampumpeag* ("white strings" of shell-beads). English speakers picked up the expression, and now a slang word for money is *wampum*.

well-groomed

Originally referring to horses, *well-groomed* means carefully tended and curried. Extended, *well-groomed* refers to humans and means to be well dressed and neat, or to things (such as a lawn) and means to be well cared for.

well-heeled

To arm a gamecock with a gaff, an artificial spur of metal used as a weapon, is to heel the bird. Hence, in American slang of the late 1800s, to furnish with anything, in particular to supply with a gun, was *to heel*. Today the reference is specifically to money, so that to be well supplied with money is to be *well-heeled*.

wet behind the ears

Many newly born animals are wet from amniotic fluid. It is said of such an animal that the last part to dry is the recessed area behind each ear. Therefore, to be immature, innocent, or naive (like a baby animal) is to be *wet* (or *not dry*) *behind the ears*. It is difficult to tell for certain whether the originators of this expression were thinking of human babies or of other animal babies. It can apply equally well to either. Users of the phrase are probably divided among those who think they are alluding to baby humans, those who think they are alluding to other baby animals, and those who do not think at all about such things.

x

The letter *x* can be traced back to an ancient Phoenician sign. The Phoenicians used it to represent our *s* sound and called it *samekh* ("fish").

yoke

A yoke is a device by which two animals, especially oxen, are joined together for pulling a plow or a vehicle. Any object resembling an animal's yoke in shape or function is a *yoke*, such as a frame fitting the neck and shoulders of a person and used for carrying a pair of buckets, baskets, or the like. Further extended, *yoke* means anything that couples or binds together, that is, a bond or a tie. *Yoke* has also been transferred to stand for the yoked animals themselves or for any pair of animals that work together.

Formerly, one of the transferred senses of the animal-related yoke was a device used around the necks of captured enemies. In ancient times, Romans and others symbolized this *yoke* by fixing two spears upright in the ground and placing another on top of them, under which captured enemies were forced to pass. Thus originated the expression *to pass under the yoke*, meaning to show submission or servitude to another.

Today *yoke* is used figuratively to mean an oppressive agency, as in "the *yoke* of marriage," or the state itself of servitude or humiliation, as in "My *yoke* is unbearable."

Animals Hidden in Words

Many words contain hidden animal names or animal-related words. The animal-related etymologies of such words are "hidden" in that the words are often borrowed from a foreign language and in that the words often no longer have anything at all to do with animals.

Many human names have animal names hidden in them. *Adler* comes from German *Adler* ("eagle"). *Adolph* is based on Old High German *athal* ("noble") plus *wolf* ("wolf"). *Arnold* goes back to Old High German *arn* ("eagle") plus *wald* ("power"), thus "strong as an eagle." *Ava* is based on Latin *avis* ("bird").

Bernard is based on the Old High German name *Berinhard*, which is a combination of *bero* or *berin* ("bear") and *hart* ("bold"), thus "bold as a bear." Variants of *Bernard* include *Barnard* (in French and English), *Bernadette* (in French), *Bernardi* and *Bernardo* (in Italian and Spanish), and *Bernhardt* (in German). Other names in which "bear" is hidden include *Baer, Bahr, Behr,* and *Behrens.*

Brock comes from the English dialectal word *brock* ("badger"). *Deborah* comes from a Hebrew word for "bee." *Farrah* comes from an Arabic word for "a wild ass." *Fisk(e)* is based on Old English *fisc* ("fish"). *Fuchs* is German for "fox." *Jonah* comes from Hebrew *yonah* ("a dove"). *Leo* is Latin, and *Leon* Greek, for "lion." *Leonard* is an Old French form of Old

High German *Lewenhart* ("strong as a lion"). *Lupino* is Italian for "little wolf."

Melissa comes from a Greek word for "bee." *Purcell* is based on Old French *pourcel* ("little pig"). *Rachel* comes from a Hebrew word for "ewe." *Spink(s)* comes from Middle English *spink* ("finch"). *Todd* comes from Old English *tod* ("fox"). *Ursula* is "little she-bear," a pet form of Latin *ursa* ("she-bear").

Some place-names, too, have animal names hidden in them. In the United States, a small bleak island in San Francisco Bay was originally called by the Spaniards *Isla de Alcatraces* ("Island of Pelicans") because of the great number of pelicans found there. In English, the name changed to the singular, *Alcatraz* ("Pelican"), and the island became the home of a federal penitentiary until it closed in 1963.

Kewanee, for a city in Illinois, comes from the name of an Indian chief, whose name means "prairie hen" in Potawatomi. *Erie*, for one of the Great Lakes, comes from the name of an Indian tribe, the Eries, whose name is based on an Iroquois word meaning "wildcat."

Mariposa, for a city in California, comes from the Spanish word for "butterfly," the city being so named for the many butterflies found there by an early Spanish expedition. *Tippecanoe*, for a river in Indiana, comes by way of folk etymology from the Potawatomi name for the river, recorded as *ki-tap-i-kon* ("buffalo fish").

Other areas of the world also have animals hidden in place-names. *Arctic*, for the region of the North Pole, comes from Greek *arktos* ("bear"). But the Greeks were not thinking of the polar bear; they were using the word in reference to the northern constellation now called, in Latin, *Ursa Major* ("Great Bear").

Canary, for a group of islands off the west coast of Africa, is based on Latin *canis* ("dog") because of the dogs reportedly found there (for more on *canary* see "Canary" in Part One). *Faroe*, for the Faroe Islands of the North Atlantic, probably comes from Danish *faar* ("sheep") plus *oe* ("island"). *Khartoum*, for a city in the Sudan, comes from the Arabic name *Ras-el-hartum* ("end of the elephant trunk"), which describes the outline of the city.

Other names with animals hidden in them include many of those for the constellations, which are generally known by their Latin names. Here are some familiar ones: *Aries* ("Ram"), *Cancer* ("Crab"), *Canis Major* ("Larger Dog"), *Canis Minor* ("Smaller Dog"), *Capricornus* ("Horned Goat"), *Cetus* ("Whale"), *Cygnus* ("Swan"), *Delphinus* ("Dolphin"), *Leo* ("Lion"), *Taurus* ("Bull"), *Ursa Major* ("Larger or Great Bear"), and *Ursa Minor* ("Smaller or Little Bear").

The above, then, are some groups of words in which animals are hidden. Below are some individual words with animal-related etymologies.

Aegis goes back to Greek *aigis* ("goatskin" or "shield of Zeus," which is often depicted as a goatskin; hence any protection). *Aigis* comes from, or is associated by folk etymology with, *aix* (stem *aig-*, "goat").

Aquiline, an adjective often used to describe a hooked nose, is based on Latin *aquila* ("eagle") because of the eagle's hooked beak.

In ancient Rome, an *auspex* was one who observed birds to divine omens for the guidance of affairs. *Auspex* is a contraction of *avispex,* from *avis* ("bird") plus *spex* ("observer," from *specere,* "to see, look at, observe"), thus "bird seer." The *auspex* was a kind of protector, hence English *auspice, auspices,* and *auspicious.*

An aviary is a place where birds are kept. The word *aviary* goes back to Latin *avis* ("bird"). When people began to fly in airplanes, it was natural to compare human flying with bird flying; thus evolved the new words *aviation* (flying), *aviator* (male flyer), and *aviatrix* (female flyer).

An ancient Scandinavian warrior noted for strength, courage, and frenzied violence in battle was called, in Old Norse, a *berserkr* ("bearshirt") because berserks (or berserkers) were so tough that they fought while wearing only a bearskin shirt instead of armor. From Old Norse *berserkr* comes English *berserk.*

Bombast comes from obsolete *bombast* ("cotton, cotton padding," hence "padded language"), which goes back to Latin *bombax* ("cotton"), a corruption of *bombyx* ("silkworm, silk"), which in turn comes from Greek *bombyx* ("silkworm"), itself of Oriental origin.

Bucolic goes back to Latin *bous* ("ox"). *Bugle* goes back to Latin *buculus* ("young ox") because the animal's horn was used as a musical instrument in ancient times.

Cajole is adapted from French *cajoler* ("to chatter like a jay in a cage, cajole"), which is an alteration of the synonymous Middle French *gaioler* (from Old North French *gaiole*, "bird-cage"). The change of *gaioler* to *cajoler* is due to the influence of French *cage* ("cage").

In French, *canard* means "duck," but in English the word has come to mean a hoax or an absurd story. This meaning probably comes from the French expression *vendre un canard à moitié* ("to half-sell a duck"). Of course, to half-sell a duck is not to sell it at all; therefore, the French expression figuratively means "to deceive, swindle." In English, the expression, with the same meaning, is shortened to *canard*.

Canine goes back to Latin *canis* ("dog").

Latin *caper* ("he-goat") yields or influences several English words. English *caper* denotes a leap, a prancing, a prank, or a crime. Although the English word goes back to Latin *caper* and is originally a reference to the playful habits of a frisky goat, it is most immediately a shortened, altered version of *capriole* (an English word adopted from French *capriole*, "leap, caper"), which means any leap or, of a trained horse, a vertical leap with a backward kick of the hind legs.

English *cabriole*, from French *cabriole* (another spelling of *capriole*, "leap, caper"), means a curved furniture leg ending in an ornamental foot (from its resemblance to the foreleg of a capering animal) or a ballet leap in which one leg is extended in midair and the other struck against it (in the manner of a capering animal).

English *cabriolet*, from French *cabriolet* (diminutive of *cabriole*, thus "little caper" or "little goatlike leap") denotes a lightweight carriage because of the bouncy movements of the vehicle. In English, *cabriolet* has also been shortened to *cab* and used in *taxicab*.

English *caprice* (hence *capricious*) is adopted from the synonymous French *caprice*, which derives from Italian *capriccio*.

Capriccio, built from *capo* ("head") plus *riccio* ("hedgehog"), is a reference to a head with hair standing straight up (like the spines of a hedgehog) in fear, hence the original sense of *capriccio* as "horror, shivering." Later, influenced by Italian *capro* ("goat," from Latin *caper*), *capriccio* developed the sense of "whim." English has, in fact, adopted not only French *caprice* but also its source, Italian *capriccio.* Today, in English, a *capriccio* is a whimsy, a caper, or an instrumental music piece in free form.

Cavalcade, cavalier, and *cavalry* go back to Latin *caballus* ("horse"). So does *chivalry.* But why does *chivalry* have an *h,* while the others do not? The answer is that the first three words are influenced by intervening Italian forms (Italian *cavallo,* "horse"), while *chivalry* is influenced by intervening French forms (French *cheval,* "horse").

Celandine, for type of plant, goes back to Greek *chelidon* ("swallow," the bird) because in ancient folklore it is said that the flower appears with the arrival of swallows and withers at their departure.

Coccyx, for a bone at the end of the vertebral column, goes back to Greek *kokkyx* ("cuckoo, coccyx") because the bone is said to resemble a cuckoo's beak.

Columbarium, for a structure of vaults lined with recesses for cinerary urns, comes from Latin *columbarium* ("dovecote"), which is based on *columba* ("dove"). The structure is obviously so named because its appearance is similar to that of a dovecote.

Columbine, for a type of plant, also goes back to Latin *columba* ("dove"), the inverted flower being said to resemble a group of doves.

Coquet, coquette, and *coquetry* are based on French *coq* ("cock"), in reference to the vain swaggering and amorous characteristics of roosters.

Coward has nothing to do with cows. The word stems from Latin *cauda* ("tail" of any animal). *Coward,* then, applies to humans the idea of a frightened animal putting its tail between its legs, or the idea of an animal "turning tail" to run away. Latin *cauda* has also developed into the musical term *coda,* meaning the last part, or "tail," of a composition.

Cynic comes from Latin *Cynicus* ("Cynic"), which goes back to Greek *kynikos* (literally "doglike," from *kyon*, "dog"), a name contemptuously applied to the Cynics because of their antisocial behavior. Diogenes, the probable founder of Cynicism, was called "The Dog." (According to *Collier's Encyclopedia*, the traditional view that *kynikos* derives from *kynosarges*, the name of a gymnasium where Antisthenes taught, is probably wrong.)

Cynosure goes back to Greek *kynosoura* ("dog's tail") because the word was early applied to the Pole Star (toward which the axis of the earth points) in the tail of the constellation *Ursa Minor* ("Smaller Bear"), hence the figurative sense of *cynosure* as any center of attraction or attention.

Dauphin, for the title of the eldest son of a king of France, is the French word for "dolphin," the fish. Before the word was applied to the son of the king, it was a proper name and a title for the lords of Viennois, France, whose coat of arms bore three dolphins.

Delphinium, for a type of plant, goes back to Greek *delphis* ("dolphin"). The plant is so named because its nectary resembles the shape of a dolphin.

Easel comes from Dutch *ezel* ("ass, donkey," which goes back to Latin *asinus*, "ass") because, like the donkey, the easel is a "beast of burden" in that it holds the artist's canvas.

Equine and *equestrian* come from Latin *equus* ("horse").

Fee goes back to Old French *fe, fief* ("fee"), which come from a Germanic source that is based on an Indo-European root meaning "cattle," hence "property," hence "wealth," hence "money."

Fungus comes from Latin *fungus* ("fungus"), which is probably a modification of Greek *spongos* ("sponge").

Geranium is based on Greek *geranion* ("small crane") because the fruit of the geranium resembles a crane's bill.

Hippic and *hippodrome* are based on Greek *hippos* ("horse").

Hippopotamus goes back to Greek *hippos ho potamios* ("horse of the river"), from *hippos* ("horse") and *potamos* ("river"). The later Greek form is *hippopotamos* ("river horse" in idiomatic English).

Isinglass comes by way of folk etymology (influenced by

English *glass*) from obsolete Dutch *huisenblas* or *huizenblas* ("sturgeon's bladder") because isinglass was originally made from the air bladders of fish.

Lupine denotes a type of plant. The word goes back to Latin *lupinus* ("wolflike"), which is based on *lupus* ("wolf"). The plant is so called because of the ancient belief that it destroys the soil. *Lupus*, for any of various diseases characterized by skin lesions, also goes back to Latin *lupus* ("wolf").

Marshal, like *constable* (see *constable* under "Animal-related Expressions"), began as a word of the stables. The Middle English word *mareschal* comes from Old French *mareschal*, which is of Germanic origin and means "horse servant," the *mare-* coming from a root meaning "horse" (compare our *mare* for a female horse) and the *-schal* coming from a root meaning "servant." In English, the word originally stood for one who tends horses. That sense is obsolete, but the word developed the extended meaning of a high official in a noble household having charge first (and naturally) of the cavalry and later of all of the military forces. *Marshal* has also come to be a military rank (as in *field marshal*). In the United States, the word applies most often to an officer who carries out court orders. The verb *to marshal* has extended from its military sense of to arrange (soldiers) for fighting to the more familiar sense of to organize (people, things, ideas) in an appropriate way.

Mukluk, for a type of boot, comes from Eskimo *muklok* ("large seal") because Eskimos made the boot from sealskin.

Muscle goes back to Latin *musculus* ("little mouse," a full-sized mouse being a *mus*), apparently because some muscles rippling under the skin look like little mice.

The word *peculiar* has a peculiar history. Latin *pecu* is "flock of sheep" or "herd of cattle." Since, in ancient times, sheep and cattle were the main forms of property and wealth, the Latin word for "money" is *pecunia* (which yields English *pecuniary* and *impecunious*), while "of private property" is *peculiaris*. From *peculiaris* comes English *peculiar*, which has gone through stages of meaning of private property, then special, and then strange. Another English word based on Latin *pecu* is the verb *to peculate*, to embezzle.

Pen for a writing instrument goes back to Latin *penna* ("feather") because early pens were made of quills, or large feathers.

The Latin word *penis* originally meant "tail" (later superseded by *cauda*), afterward "male copulatory organ." The word is the base of several English words. The English word *penis*, of course, comes from Latin *penis*. *Pencil* goes back to Latin *penicillus* ("paintbrush, pencil," literally "little tail"), which is a diminutive of *peniculus* ("brush," literally "little tail," because brushes were made of oxtails and horsetails), itself a diminutive of *penis* ("tail"). *Penicillin* comes from New Latin *Penicillium* (the name of a genus of fungi), which comes from Latin *penicillum* (neuter of the masculine *penicillus* ("paintbrush") because of the brushlike ends of the conidiophores of the fungi.

Pica meaning a craving to eat such unnatural food as chalk or paint comes from Latin *pica* ("magpie") because of the bird's omnivorous feeding. *Pica* also stands for a size of printer's type, probably named after Medieval Latin *pica* ("collection of church rules"), perhaps in reference to the type used in printing the book, though no such version is actually known. The book itself was probably named after Latin *pica* ("magpie"), perhaps because the book's black-and-white appearance resembled the colors of the bird.

Piscary, for a fishery, and *piscator*, for an angler, go back to Latin *piscis* ("fish").

Puce, for a color variously described as brownish purple or dark red, comes from French *puce* ("flea, flea color"), which goes back to Latin *pulex* ("flea").

Purple goes back to Latin *purpura* ("purple"), which comes from Greek *porphura* ("shellfish yielding a purple dye"), which is of Semitic origin.

Queue is adopted from French *queue* ("tail," hence "line"), itself from Old French *cue, coue* ("tail"), which come from Latin *cauda* ("tail").

Rostrum comes from Latin *rostrum* ("beak" of a bird or "snout" of an animal) because in ancient Rome *rostrum* ("beak") was transferred to the pointed prow of a ship, and then such *rostra* ("beaks" of ships) were used to decorate the speakers' platform (called the *Rostra*) in the Forum.

Scrofula, for a type of disease that enlarges glands, comes from Medieval Latin *scrofulae* ("glandular swellings," literally "little pigs"), which goes back to Latin *scrofa* ("breeding sow"), the swellings evidently reminding early observers of little pigs.

Toreador is adopted from Spanish *toreador* ("bullfighter"), which is based on *toro* ("bull"), which goes back to Latin *taurus* ("bull").

Tragedy derives from Greek *tragoidia* ("tragedy," literally "goat song"), which combines *tragos* ("goat") and *oide* ("song"). The original reason for this expression is uncertain, but the word may refer to the satyrs (half human, half goat) represented by the chorus in early plays. Another theory is that *tragoidia* refers to the goatskins worn by early actors. Still another idea is that the word refers to the custom of awarding a prize of a goat to the best reciter. Perhaps two or all of these influences combined.

Ukulele, based on Hawaiian *uku* ("flea") and *lele* ("to jump"), means "jumping flea."

Vermicelli, for pasta made in thin strings, is the plural of Italian *vermicello* ("little worm"), which goes back to Latin *vermis* ("worm"), the food being so called because of its appearance.

Vermilion and *vermeil* go back to Late Latin *vermiculus* (literally "little worm," specifically "kermes," the dried bodies of certain female insects used as a red dyestuff, hence "scarlet"), which is a diminutive of Latin *vermis* ("worm"). *Vermis* is also the source of *vermicular, vermiculation,* and other squirmy *vermi-* words.

Wilderness goes back to Old English unattested *wild(d)eornes* ("wilderness"), a compound of *wilde* ("wild") and *deor* (formerly any "animal") and *-nes* ("place"), thus "wild-animal place."

Zodiac goes back to Latin *zodiacus* ("zodiac"), which comes from Greek *zoidiakos kyklos* ("zodiac circle," literally "circle of animals"), which is based on *zoion* ("animal").

Animal Sounds

Many verbs referring to animal sounds have been extended to apply to other sounds or types of behavior.

to bark

To make the short, harsh cry of a dog. *To bark* goes back through Middle English *berken* ("to bark") to Old English *beorcan* ("to bark") to an Indo-European root meaning "to growl." Extended to humans, *to bark* means to speak or cry out with a tone that suggests the sharp, explosive sound of a dog.

A dog howling aimlessly at night is not likely to accomplish anything worthwhile. Similarly, among humans, to protest against something without getting any practical results is *to bark* (or *bay*) *at the moon*.

A person who stands before a theater or a sideshow of a carnival and shouts to attract passersby is called, because of the characteristic tone of the person's voice, a *barker*.

During America's pioneer days, a common nighttime activity was hunting for raccoons. A "coon dog" was let loose to hunt for the animals. After it trapped a raccoon in a tree, the dog was supposed to stay at the foot of the tree and bark until the master came. But on a dark night the dog could make a mistake and bark up the wrong tree. The raccoon, of course, would then escape. It is now figuratively said that to be on any wrong course of action is *to bark up the wrong tree.*

to bay

To utter a deep, prolonged bark or howl, especially of hounds closing in on prey. *To bay* goes back to Old French *bayer, abayer* ("to bark"), which may come from an unattested Vulgar Latin word imitative of yawning, in reference to the opening of the barking dog's mouth. Extended to humans, *to bay* means to shout or utter in deep, prolonged tones. (For *to bay at the moon* see *to bark at the moon* above.) Other senses of the verb *to bay* are (of dogs) to pursue with barking and (of humans) to hold at bay, which are influenced by the noun *bay* in the phrases *at bay* and *to bay.*

The noun *bay* is apparently a confusion of two words. The phrase *to hold at bay* is probably originally a translation of the Old French phrase *tenir a bay,* in which *bay* refers to a state of suspense indicated by the open mouth. But *to stand at bay* and *to be brought to bay* mean to be at close quarters with barking dogs, in which *bay* comes from obsolete English *abay* (from Old French *abai,* "barking").

The primary sense of the English noun *bay* is, then, a deep, prolonged barking of an attacking dog, especially a chorus of such barking when dogs have trapped an animal, hence the encounter itself between hounds and their prey. Such an encounter has generated several common expressions that combine the French and the English senses of *bay* mentioned above. In these expressions, *bay* refers to the position of either the hunted animal or the pursuing hounds.

The position of the hunted animal is indicated in the phrase *to stand* (or *be*) *at bay.* The effective action of the hunted animal is indicated in the phrase *to hold* (or *keep*) *at bay* (the hounds). The action of the hounds is indicated in the phrases *to hold* (or *have*) *at bay* and *to bring to bay* (the hunted animal).

Figuratively, *bay* is the position of one unable to retreat and forced to face danger. The reverse is also true: *bay* is the position of one checked. All of the above phrases have been figuratively applied to humans.

to bellow

To emit the loud, deep, prolonged roar of a bull. *To bellow* goes back to Old English *bylgan* ("to bellow"), which is based on an Indo-European root meaning "to make a loud noise, roar." Among humans, to speak or shout in a loud, deep, unrestrained voice is *to bellow*.

to bleat

To utter the characteristic cry of a sheep, a goat, or a calf. *To bleat* derives from Old English *blaetan* ("to bleat"), which is based on an Indo-European imitative root meaning "to howl." Extended to humans, *to bleat* means to whimper or whine, to talk complainingly, or to talk without proper consideration.

to bray

To utter the loud, harsh cry of a donkey. *To bray* goes back to Old French *braire* ("to cry aloud"), which is probably based on a Celtic imitative root meaning "to cry, make a grating noise." The verb is sometimes applied contemptuously to the human voice. Harsh-sounding wind, thunder, musical instruments, and so on, are also said *to bray*.

to buzz

To make the low droning sound of a bee. *To buzz* is imitative of the noise made by the insect. Extended to humans, *to buzz* means to make an indistinct murmuring sound. And as bees or other insects buzz while they fly, so a person or a thing moving in a hurry is said *to buzz*. To leave quickly is *to buzz off*.

to cackle

To make the sharp, broken noise of a hen, especially just after it lays an egg. *To cackle* comes from Middle English *cakelen* ("to cackle"), which is based on an Indo-European root imitative of the hen's sound. It is figuratively said of humans that to talk or laugh in a noisy, broken way is *to cackle*. And to chatter, especially loudly or fussily about one's petty achievements (as a hen seems to brag about her egg) is *to cackle*.

to chatter

To utter a rapid succession of short sounds of a bird or an animal. *To chatter* is of imitative origin. Extended to humans, *to chatter* means to talk rapidly or idly. To make any kind of sound from rapidly repeated contacts (as the teeth often do from cold or fear) is *to chatter*.

to cheep

To utter the faint, shrill sounds of a young bird. *To cheep* is of imitative origin. Extended to humans, *to cheep* means to make a small sound, to utter a word—often in the negative, as in "She didn't even *cheep*."

to chirp

To make the short, sharp sounds of a small bird or an insect (such as a cricket). *To chirp* is of imitative origin. Extended to humans, *to chirp* means to speak in a manner resembling the chirping of birds, especially in lively tones.

To chirrup has evolved from *to chirp*, with which it is synonymous, though *to chirrup* (perhaps through the influence of *cheer up*) often implies a livelier and more sustained effect. *To chirrup* also has a special sense: to make a sound by sucking in air through compressed lips (to urge on a horse).

to chitter

To utter the sharp, thin sounds of a bird. *To chitter* is a variant of *to chatter* (see *to chatter* above). In British dialectal usage, *to chitter* means to shiver or (of the teeth) to chatter, especially from cold. In general usage, the word is found most often in the noun form *chitter-chatter*, an extension (influenced by *chit-chat*) of *chatter*, meaning light talk.

to cluck

To make the characteristic sound of a hen. *To cluck* is imitative of the hen's noise and is probably influenced in form by Latin *glocire* ("to cluck"), which is also imitative. The hen is noted for her excited clucking to call her chicks. To make any similar sound, such as a clicking sound with the tongue, is *to cluck*. And since the hen's clucking characteristically represents her concern about her chicks, to express any kind of interest or concern is *to cluck*.

The hen has a low level of intelligence. Therefore, since the word *cluck* is associated with the hen, a stupid or naive person is sometimes called a *cluck*, commonly a *dumb cluck*.

to coo

To make the soft murmuring sound of a dove or a pigeon. *To coo* is of imitative origin. Extended to humans, *to coo* means to utter a soft sound of affection or pleasure (as of an infant), sometimes seeking to placate. *To coo* also means to talk fondly or amorously (see *bill and coo* under "Bill" in Part One).

to croak

To make the deep, harsh sound characteristic of a frog, a raven, or certain other animals. *To croak* is of imitative origin. Extended to humans, *to croak* means to speak in a low, harsh voice.

The animal croaking sound is usually thought to be sad or eerie. Furthermore, the raven, which has a croaking sound, has long been superstitiously regarded as a prophet of evil. Therefore, when a person speaks about sad things or predicts evil, he is said *to croak*.

A dying person sometimes makes a gurgling sound (the death rattle). That sound has been compared with the croaking of animals. The sound is also, of course, a prediction of a sad event—death. Therefore, to die (with or without the death rattle itself) is *to croak*.

A *croaker* is anyone who croaks. Most commonly, though, *croaker* refers to a doctor, who must constantly deal with people who are going to die *(croak)*.

to crow

To make the cock-a-doodle-doo sound of a rooster. *To crow* goes back to Old English *crawan* ("to crow"), which is based on an Indo-European imitative root meaning "to cry hoarsely." Extended to humans, *to crow* means to utter a loud sound of joy.

Roosters are known for their loud crowing after they have gained a victory, as in a cockfight. They appear to be boasting. Therefore, to brag loudly is *to crow*, often *to crow over*.

to gobble

To make the characteristic guttural noise of a male turkey. *To gobble* is of imitative origin, though perhaps influenced in form by the earlier *to gobble*, to swallow hurriedly, or *to gabble*, to jabber. To make a sound or to talk in a manner resembling the turkey's sound is *to gobble*, as in "He liked *to gobble* objections."

Gobbledygook (or *gobbledegook*) means verbose and unintelligible language. The expression was coined by Maury Maverick, grandson of the man who gave us the bovine-related *maverick* (see "Maverick" in Part One). He was a Texas politician who used the word in 1944 as a name for Washington's pompous, windy, vague bureaucratic language. He said he was referring to a Texas turkey that was always "gobbledygobbling and strutting with ludicrous pomposity. At the end of this gobble there was a sort of gook." The word has since extended its meaning, so that the specialized language of a group or, in fact, any meaningless jumble of words is now called *gobbledygook*.

to growl

To utter the low guttural sound, especially in anger, of various animals, particularly a dog. (An earlier use of the word, referring to the bowels and meaning to rumble, was extremely rare; therefore, the continuity of that word with modern *growl* is uncertain. In any case, the record clearly shows that modern uses of the verb *to growl* began with references to, and extensions of, the animal sense of the word.) *To growl* is of imitative origin. To make a sound similar to the growling of an animal (as, for example, thunder does) is *to growl*. Of humans, it is said that to speak angrily is *to growl*.

to grunt

To utter the natural throat noise of a hog. *To grunt* comes from Middle English *grunten* ("to grunt"), itself from Old English *grunnettan*, a frequentative of *grunian* ("to grunt"), which is based on an Indo-European imitative root meaning "to grunt." To make a sound (as in annoyance or effort) or to speak in a manner similar to the grunting of a hog is *to grunt*, as in "She *grunted* her disapproval."

to honk

To utter the characteristic cry of a goose. *To honk* comes from the noun *honk*, which is of imitative origin. To make a noise resembling a goose's cry (such as the sound of various horns) is *to honk*.

to howl

Of a dog or a wolf, to utter a loud, prolonged, sad cry in which a $\bar{u}$ sound prevails. *To howl* is based on an Indo-European imitative root meaning "to howl." Among humans, to make a sound similar to the animal's howl, especially to wail or lament with pain, is *to howl*. Other things (such as the wind) can also *howl*. Extended, *to howl* means to go on a spree or a rampage.

The noun *howl* means an animal yell. Extended, *howl* means a wail, an outcry of rage or disappointment, a complaint, or something that provokes laughter.

to low

To utter the deep, sustained sound of cattle. *To low* is an older synonym for *to moo* (see *to moo* below). The verb goes back to Old English *hlowan* ("to low"), which is based on an Indo-European imitative root meaning "to shout, cry out." To make a sound reminiscent of the mooing of cattle is *to low*, as in "He would *low* with contentment."

to meow

To utter the characteristic cry of a cat. *To meow* is a newer synonym for *to mew* (see *to mew* below). The verb is of imitative origin. To make a spiteful or malicious remark is *to meow*.

to mew

To utter the characteristic sound of a cat. *To mew* is an older synonym for *to meow* (see *to meow* above). The verb is of imitative origin. Literally or figuratively, *to mew* is now found less often than *to meow*, at least in the United States.

to moo

To make the characteristic throat noise of cattle. *To moo* is a newer synonym for *to low* (see *to low* above). The verb is of imitative origin. To utter with a sound resembling the lowing of an ox or a cow is *to moo*, as in "They *moo* their song."

to neigh

To utter the loud, prolonged cry of a horse. *To neigh* goes back to Old English *hnaegan* ("to neigh"), of imitative origin. To utter as if by neighing is *to neigh*, as in "He *neighed* his approval."

to peep

To make the soft and gentle little chirps of a young bird. *To peep* is of imitative origin and is influenced in form by Latin *pipare* ("to peep"). Extended to humans, *to peep* means to utter the slightest sound.

to purr

To utter the characteristic sound of a contented cat. *To purr* is of imitative origin. Extended to humans, *to purr* means to speak in a soft, murmuring voice. Other things that make a purrlike sound, such as a good engine, are also said *to purr*.

to quack

To make the characteristic sound of a duck. *To quack* is of imitative origin. Extended to humans, *to quack* means to utter a harsh sound resembling that of a duck.

An obsolete term for a person who pretends to have medical skill that he does not really have is *quacksalver*, that is, one who quacks (boasts) loudly about his salves (medicines). *Quacksalver* is adopted from obsolete Dutch *quacksalver* of the same meaning. (Some authorities say that the *quack* in the Dutch word may originally have had a different sense, for example, *quac* meaning "unguent," but that folk etymology changed the sense to *quack* meaning "to make a harsh sound like a duck's.") Today the word is shortened to *quack*, and the meaning of the expression has broadened, so that a person who pretends to have any skill or knowledge that he does not really have is called a *quack.*

to snarl

Of a dog, to growl angrily while snapping or gnashing the teeth. *To snarl* is a frequentative of the earlier *snar,* which is based on an Indo-European root of various verbs for making nasal-related noises. To express angrily in surly language is *to snarl.*

to sneer

Originally of a horse, to snort. *To sneer* is based on an Indo-European root of various verbs for making nasal-related noises. The later (modern) sense of *to sneer* (probably influenced by the facial appearance of a snorting horse) is to smile or laugh with a face of scorn, hence to speak or write in a scornful manner.

to snore

Originally of a horse, to snort. *To snore* is based on an Indo-European root of various verbs for making nasal-related noises. The modern sense of *to snore* (influenced by the noise of a snorting horse) is to breathe during sleep with a harsh, rough noise due to vibration of the soft palate.

to snort

Of a horse, to make a loud, harsh sound by forcing air violently through the nose. *To snort* is based on an Indo-European root of various verbs for making nasal-related noises. Transferred to things, *to snort* means to emit explosive sounds (such as those of a railroad engine) resembling animal snorts. Extended to humans, *to snort* means to express contempt, anger, or surprise by a snort. To utter with or as if with snorts is also *to snort,* as in "'Drop dead!' he *snorted."*

to twitter

Of a bird, to utter a succession of light, tremulous sounds, or chirps. *To twitter* is of imitative origin. Extended to humans, *to twitter* means to talk rapidly in a chattering manner, to giggle, or to tremble.

to yap

To utter the sharp bark of a dog. *To yap* is of imitative origin. The verb is close in meaning to *to yelp* (see *to yelp* below). Extended to humans, *to yap* means to speak in a shrill and snappish way or to talk idly.

The noun *yap* originally referred to the dog itself, then to the dog's sound. Extended, *yap* means chatter, an ignorant person, or (in slang) the mouth.

to yelp

To utter the shrill cry of a dog. *To yelp* comes from Middle English *yelpen* ("to cry aloud"), itself from Old English *gielpan* ("to boast noisily"), which is based on an Indo-European root meaning "to cry out." *To yelp* is close in meaning to *to yap* (see *to yap* above). Extended to humans, *to yelp* means to call or cry out sharply.

Animal Sounds in Various Languages

Different groups of people hear the same animal sounds in different ways. In some cases, the difference is not too great. English speakers, for example, hear the cow's sound as *moo*. In French, the word is *meuh;* in Spanish and Russian, *mu*. The English word for the cat's sound is *meow*, while in French it is *miaou;* in Italian, *miao;* and in German, *miau*.

But other languages do not agree. *Meow* in Japanese, for example, is a sound like *nya-nya;* and in Arabic, *nau-nau*.

The English *cock-a-doodle-doo* of the rooster is *cocorico* in French, *quiquiriqui* in Spanish, *kikiriki* in German, *kukureku* in Russian, *ko-ko* or *qee-qee* in Arabic, *kokekkoko* in Japanese, and *cuc-cu* in Vietnamese.

English has *gobble-gobble* for the turkey's sound, though few other languages have bothered to imitate the animal.

On the other hand, English has no real imitation of the barnyard hen. English *cluck* is really not close. In French, the hen says *cot-cot;* in Arabic, *qa-qa;* in Chinese, *ko-ko-ko;* in Japanese, *kukku;* in Vietnamese, *cuc-tac;* and in ancient Latin, *co-co* or *co-co-co*.

English also has no imitation of the horse's neigh. In Italian, though, the horse says *ih-ih-ih-ih-ih;* in Arabic, *hem-hem;* and in Japanese, *hi-hin*.

An English mouse says *squeak-squeak;* but a French one

says *kwee-kwee*, a Spanish one *chee-chee*, and a Russian one *psk-psk*.

The English *quack-quack* of the duck is *couac-couac* or *coin-coin* (pronounced like *kwan-kwan*) in French. A German duck agrees with the English in saying *quack-quack*. Fairly close are Spanish with *cuac-cuac*, Italian with *qua-qua*, Russian with *kva-kva*, and Vietnamese with *cac-cac*. But quite different are Japanese *ga-ga*, Arabic *bat-bat*, Mandarin Chinese *ya-ya*, and South China's Cantonese *ap-ap*.

English chicks and small birds *peep* and *chirp*. But in Italian they say *pio-pio*; in Rumanian, *piu-piu*; and in French, *cui-cui*.

The donkey's sound in English is *hee-haw*. In French, it is *hi-han*; in Italian and Chinese, *i-o*; in German and Russian, *i-a*; and in Arabic, *ham-ham* or *hee-hee*.

The English pig's *oink-oink* is *oui-oui* (which also means "yes-yes") in French, *khru-khru* in Russian, and *quits-quits* in Rumanian.

The animal that has the widest range of differences in the imitations of its sound is the dog. The main reason is probably that there are so many different breeds of domesticated dogs around the world. English speakers hear the dog saying *arf-arf*, *bow-wow*, *woof-woof*, or *yip-yip*. In French, the sound is *wah-wah*; in Italian, *bu-bu*; in Spanish, *guau-guau* or *jau-jau* (pronounced like *how-how*); in German, *hau-hau* or *wau-wau*; in Russian, *vas-vas* or *vaf-vaf*; in Vietnamese, *gau-gau*; in Turkish, *hov-hov*; in Chinese, *wang-wang*; in Japanese, *wan-wan*; and in ancient Sanskrit (of India), *bhuk-bhuk*.

Selected Bibliography

The American Heritage Dictionary of the English Language. Boston: Houghton Mifflin Co., 1979.

The Bible. King James Version.

Brewer, Ebenezer Cobham. *Brewer's Dictionary of Phrase and Fable.* Revised by Ivor H. Evans. New York: Harper & Row, Publishers, 1970.

Ciardi, John. *A Browser's Dictionary.* New York: Harper & Row, Publishers, 1980.

Collier's Encyclopedia. New York: Macmillan Educational Corporation, 1979.

Collins, V. H. *A Book of English Idioms.* London: Longmans, Green, and Co., 1957.

Cooper, J.C. *An Illustrated Encyclopaedia of Traditional Symbols.* London: Thames and Hudson, 1978.

Craigie, Sir William A., and James R. Hulbert, editors. *A Dictionary of American English on Historical Principles.* Four volumes. Chicago: University of Chicago Press, 1936-44.

The Encyclopedia Americana. Danbury, Connecticut: Grolier Inc., 1981.

Flexner, Stuart Berg. *I Hear America Talking.* New York: Van Nostrand Reinhold Co., 1976.

Klein, Ernest. *A Comprehensive Etymological Dictionary of the English Language.* New York: Elsevier Publishing Co., 1971.

Kolatch, Alfred J. *The Jonathan David Dictionary of First Names.* Middle Village, New York: Jonathan David Publishers, Inc., 1980.

Leach, Maria, editor. *Funk & Wagnalls Standard Dictionary of Folklore, Mythology, and Legend.* New York: Funk & Wagnalls, 1972.

Mathews, Mitford M. *American Words.* Cleveland: The World Publishing Co., 1959.

————, editor. *A Dictionary of Americanisms on Historical Principles.* Two volumes. Chicago: University of Chicago Press, 1951.

Mencken, H.L. *The American Language.* Fourth edition. New York: Alfred A. Knopf, 1936.

————. *The American Language.* Supplement One. New York: Alfred A. Knopf, 1945.

————. *The American Language.* Supplement Two. New York: Alfred A. Knopf, 1948.

Morris, William and Mary. *Morris Dictionary of Word and Phrase Origins.* New York: Harper & Row, Publishers, 1977.

Onions, C.T., editor. *The Oxford Dictionary of English Etymology.* Oxford, England: Oxford University Press, 1966.

The Oxford English Dictionary. Twelve volumes and supplement. Oxford, England: Oxford University Press, 1933. *A Supplement to the Oxford English Dictionary.* Edited by R. W. Burchfield. Two volumes. Oxford, England: Oxford University Press, 1972-76.

Partridge, Eric. *Origins: A Short Etymological Dictionary of Modern English.* Fourth edition. New York: Macmillan Publishing Co., 1966.

Pei, Mario. *What's in a Word?* New York: Hawthorn Books, 1968.

The Random House Dictionary of the English Language. New York: Random House, 1966.

Reaney, P.H. *The Origin of English Surnames.* London: Routledge and Kegan Paul, 1967.

Room, Adrian. *Place-Names of the World.* Totowa, New Jersey: Rowman and Littlefield, 1974.

Smith, William George, compiler. *The Oxford Dictionary of English Proverbs.* Third edition. Revised by F. P. Wilson. Oxford, England: Oxford University Press, 1970.

Spears, Richard A. *Slang and Euphemism.* Middle Village, New York: Jonathan David Publishers, Inc., 1981.

Stevenson, Burton, editor. *The Home Book of Proverbs, Maxims, and Familiar Phrases.* New York: The Macmillan Co., 1948.

Stewart, George R. *American Place-Names.* New York: Oxford University Press, 1970.

Taylor, Archer, and Bartlett Jere Whiting. *A Dictionary of American Proverbs and Proverbial Phrases, 1820-1880.* Cambridge, Massachusetts: Harvard University Press, 1958.

Urdang, Laurence, editorial director. *Picturesque Expressions: A Thematic Dictionary.* Detroit: Gale Research Co., 1980.

Webster's New Collegiate Dictionary. Springfield, Massachusetts: G. & C. Merriam Co., 1977.

Webster's New World Dictionary of the American Language. Second College Edition. Cleveland and New York: William Collins + World Publishing Co., Inc., 1976.

Webster's Third New International Dictionary of the English Language. Springfield, Massachusetts: G. & C. Merriam Co., 1961.

Wentworth, Howard, and Stuart Berg Flexner, compilers and editors. *Dictionary of American Slang.* Second edition. New York: Thomas Y. Crowell Co., 1975.

Index